Sewn in the Sweatshops of Marx

Sewn in the Sweatshops of Marx

Beuys, Warhol, Klein, Duchamp

THIERRY DE DUVE

Translated by Rosalind E. Krauss

University of Chicago Press :: CHICAGO AND LONDON

Thierry de Duve is an art historian, critic, and curator.
His publications in English include *Kant after Duchamp* and
Clement Greenberg between the Lines.

The University of Chicago Press, Chicago 60637
The University of Chicago Press, Ltd., London
© 2012 by Thierry de Duve
All rights reserved. Published 2012.

21 20 19 18 17 16 15 14 13 12   1 2 3 4 5

ISBN-13: 978-0-226-92237-9 (cloth)
ISBN-13: 978-0-226-92238-6 (paper)
ISBN-13: 978-0-226-92239-3 (e-book)
ISBN-10: 0-226-92237-5 (cloth)
ISBN-10: 0-226-92238-3 (paper)
ISBN-10: 0-226-92239-1 (e-book)

Library of Congress Cataloging-in-Publication Data

Duve, Thierry de.
 [Cousus de fil d'or. English]
 Sewn in the sweatshops of Marx : Beuys, Warhol, Klein, Duchamp / Thierry
de Duve ; Translated by Rosalind E. Krauss.
     pages cm
  ISBN 978-0-226-92237-9 (cloth : alkaline paper) — ISBN 978-0-226-92238-6
(paperback : alkaline paper) — ISBN 978-0-226-92239-3 (e-book) —
ISBN 0-226-92237-5 (cloth : alkaline paper) — ISBN 0-226-92238-3 (paperback :
alkaline paper) — ISBN 0-226-92239-1 (e-book)   1. Art, Modern—20th century.
2. Beuys, Joseph. 3. Warhol, Andy, 1928–1987. 4. Klein, Yves, 1928–1962.
5. Duchamp, Marcel, 1887–1968.   I. Krauss, Rosalind E., translator. II. Title.
  N6490.D8813 2012
  709.04—dc23

                                                            2012011387

Contents

Preface 2009

Milton produced *Paradise Lost* for the same reason a
silkworm produces silk. It was an activity of his nature.

KARL MARX, *Capital, Book IV*

If the silkworm were to spin in order to provide for its
existence as a caterpillar, it would be a perfect wage-worker.

KARL MARX, *Wage-Labor and Capital*

This book started as a commission—of the kind you instinctively tell
yourself: there is trouble ahead, an irresistible incentive. In December 1987, a French publisher approached me on behalf of a Parisian
art gallery with a specific request. The gallery in question was soon
to stage an exhibition gathering works by Joseph Beuys, Marcel Duchamp, Yves Klein, and Andy Warhol. Would I write an essay linking
those four artists together? I politely declined the invitation, on the
grounds that catalogue essays were by principle not critical of the
artist, and I might be very critical of Yves Klein.[1] But when the reply
came that I was to produce an independent *book* published merely
on the occasion of the gallery show and that I would be granted all
liberty, I said I would think it over. I didn't sleep much that night,
for I was hooked. In my insomnia, a red thread imposed itself that
would indeed, and convincingly, link the four artists together, as
well as articulate my own writing to its material circumstances:
money. Not money per se, but money as symptomatic of a phenomenon that I had an inkling was constitutive of modernity, and which
our four artists had brought to a close, completed, terminated: the
perfect mapping of the aesthetic field onto that of political economy.

---

1. See Postface 2009, below.

You might say I espoused Walter Benjamin's intuition that politics and economics had displaced religion as the relevant interpretant (in Peirce's sense) for art, but with a retrospective twist that made Benjamin more a part of the phenomenon he analyzed than its outside analyst.

The next day I called the publisher and told him I accepted the commission. Four months later I sent him the manuscript, and he refused it. I had written critical things about Yves Klein, and the "book" was in effect a catalogue exhibition in disguise. So much for my naiveté.

I waited a year and then offered the manuscript to a publishing house whose policy I felt affinity with. *Art Edition* was happy to publish it (my gratitude to the late Jean-Louis Maubant for this). We gave the book the untranslatable title *Cousus de fil d'or: Beuys, Warhol, Klein, Duchamp.*[2] As a literal rendering conveying what my red thread had been, "Sewn with Gold Thread" is fine, but it doesn't conjure up the French *cousu de fil blanc*, a phrase that intimates blatantly transparent reasoning and means something like "worn on one's sleeve." The reason for that innuendo had to do with the tongue-in-cheek avowal of banality I wanted the title to connote. If its English adaptation, *Sewn in the Sweatshops of Marx: Beuys, Warhol, Klein, Duchamp*, suggests that some gross appeal to Marxism, too gross to be taken at face value, connects these four very different artists, then it wears its own deception on its sleeve, and it is not a bad title. But I should not give away why I think so.

For quite a while the English version of *Cousus de fil d'or* did not have a title because it did not require one. Having read the manuscript and upon hearing why the publisher refused it, Rosalind Krauss offered to issue it in four installments in *October* magazine. Moreover, she did the translation herself.[3] My gratitude to her is matched only by my gratitude to Susan Bielstein, who has offered to

2. *Cousus de fil d'or: Beuys, Warhol, Klein, Duchamp* (Villeurbanne, France: Art Edition, 1990).

3. "Joseph Beuys, or The Last of the Proletarians," *October*, no. 45 (Summer 1988): 47–62 (reprinted in Claudia Mesch and Viola Michely, eds., *Joseph Beuys: The Reader* [London: I. B. Tauris, 2007]); "Andy Warhol, or The Machine Perfected," *October*, no. 48 (Spring 1989): 3–14; "Yves Klein, or The Dead Merchant," *October*,

harbor several books of mine at the University of Chicago Press, and who has made me wonder why I waited twenty-one years to reunite those four *October* articles in their original book form. Here they are, with only minor retouches to the translation and none of any significance to the original manuscript.

In the month that followed my acceptance of the commission, I frantically read or reread all of Karl Marx's economic writings, from the Manuscripts of 1844 to *Capital*. I took notes, many. Then I filed all this away and wrote the book in three months, without a footnote. No doubt it suffers from this haste; whether it also gains from the speed and energy the reading of Marx imparted is for the reader to judge. Marx really is its red thread—which, to be fair, doesn't make it a Marxist (or an anti-Marxist) book for all that, but something "Marxian" came together for me in the first months of 1988. I was certainly not the first intellectual to realize that if Marx was as young as ever, it was not for the predictive but for the explanatory value of his writings. For many, this was cause of suffering. For me, it became an uncanny source of exhilaration: Marx can still help us make sense of modernity—in art and elsewhere—without obliging us to endorse or, for that matter, reject, mourn, or lament his political hopes. Because his writings cannot totally be stripped of their utopianism, they offer themselves as a projection plane for modernity's many unfulfilled promises, as a map, a translation device, an interpretant (again in Peirce's sense). Marx helped me treat the disenchantment with modernity that characterizes so much contemporary thinking with the same cruel gaiety with which the thinkers of the Enlightenment treated what Max Weber has called the disenchantment of the world. The choice is not between postmodern melancholy and postmodern*ist* cynicism. When myths and utopias are read against the grain of their authors' wishes, they release new, liberating meanings and feelings. My exhilaration in reading Marx in the first months of 1988 resembles Kant's enthusiasm at a remove when he was confronted with the French Revolution. Kant did not rejoice at the sight of the revolution; he rejoiced at the sight of the enthusiasm for the revolution among those who had more to

no. 49 (Summer 1989): 73–90; and "Marcel Duchamp, or The *Phynancier* of Modern Life," *October*, no. 52 (Summer 1990): 61–75.

lose than to gain from it. Similarly, studying Marx in 1988 with the results of Marxist utopias in mind could hardly have been enthralling. But that Marx's ideas had been effectively enthralling, for so many people who were ultimately to suffer from them, was and still is a sign—and not one that should yield melancholy or cynicism. I read it, despite every betrayal, as a sign of hope—perhaps not the hope that a revolution finally occurs that will not be betrayed, but more soberly, the hope that the Enlightenment will, at last, really be brought to fruition.

Sewn in the Sweatshops of Marx: Beuys, Warhol, Klein, Duchamp is not a book on Marx, though it is literally suspended from the two quotations of Marx in the above epigraph. The book is, and is not, a book on the four artists listed in the title. In the rather short chapters composing the book, I shall of necessity remain elliptical in the survey of their oeuvre and allusive in the discussion of particular works. What the book is mainly about is the mapping of the aesthetic field onto that of political economy, a phenomenon that I think deserves to be seen as constitutive of modernity, in art. Beuys, Warhol, Klein, and Duchamp are singled out because they provide an exemplary retrospective viewpoint on that phenomenon, inasmuch as they show the mapping of the two fields as accomplished to the point of perfect congruence or complete overlap.

Skeptical readers may remind me that Beuys, Warhol, Klein, and Duchamp were not singled out by me but by the publisher who commissioned the book and then refused it. That's right. I was lucky. If I were to rewrite and expand the book (which I shall not do), I would add two artists and pair them critically: Joseph Beuys / Marcel Broodthaers, Andy Warhol / Marcel Duchamp, Yves Klein / Piero Manzoni. The latter makes a cameo appearance that indicates where this might take me.

Joseph Beuys, or The Last of the Proletarians

Overcome by an illness that took hold of him—like a statue—by the feet, Joseph Beuys died on January 21, 1986, after having installed in the Capodimonte Museum in Naples what should be seen as more than just his last exhibition: his testament. On the walls were seven gold-leafed monochromes, measuring the height of a man and asymmetrically arranged: four on the right-hand wall, one on the far wall, two on the wall at the left. In the room stood two vitrines, or rather, glass caskets—one displaced to a position near the left-hand wall, the other right in the middle. The first contained the pathetic implements of a transient or bum, these arranged in a vaguely anthropomorphic manner: a backpack serving as head; two bronze canes, one rolled in felt, doubling as arms; two rolls of fat and a roll of leather bound with twine standing for chest; and a slab of lard for legs. Alongside this dismembered body ran a bronze crutch to which were attached two large electrical clamps. There lay the artist as vagabond, as itinerant clown, encumbered with his meager supplies and limping down the road to exile: Oedipus at Colonnus.

In the central casket the portrait was more composed, tragic, majestic: Oedipus Rex. A cast head (the same that topped *Strassenbahnhaltestelle* at the 1982 Venice Biennale), its mouth agape as for a last death-cry, protruded from a greatcoat made of hare skin and lined in blue silk, at the feet of which was set the conch shell of a hoped-for rebirth. Two cymbals (used in the performance *Titus/Iphigenia*) stood in at the place where in the other coffin the electric clamps with their supporting crutch were located. There lay the artist as tragic monarch, clad in the regalia of his office. The installation was, moreover, titled *Palazzo Regale*.

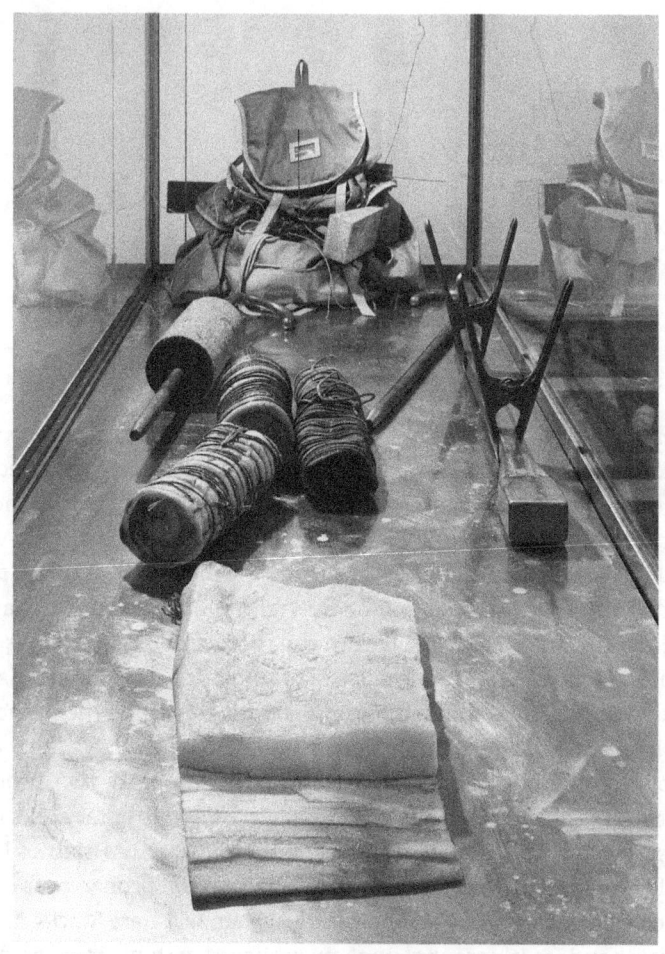

Joseph Beuys, *Palazzo Regale*, 1985. Museo di Capodimonte, Naples. Photo: Claudio Abate. © 2012 Artists Rights Society (ARS), New York / VG Bild-Kunst, Bonn

It is as vain to try to choose between the two images of himself the artist has wished to bequeath us as it would be mistaken to think that—as if retracing Beuys's career—they map a trajectory from the marginality of his beginnings to the triumph of his end. Like the faces of Janus, the two *gisants* are inseparable. And they are mutually indispensable for understanding what Beuys, throughout his whole life as an artist, wished to incarnate. The ruler and the tramp,

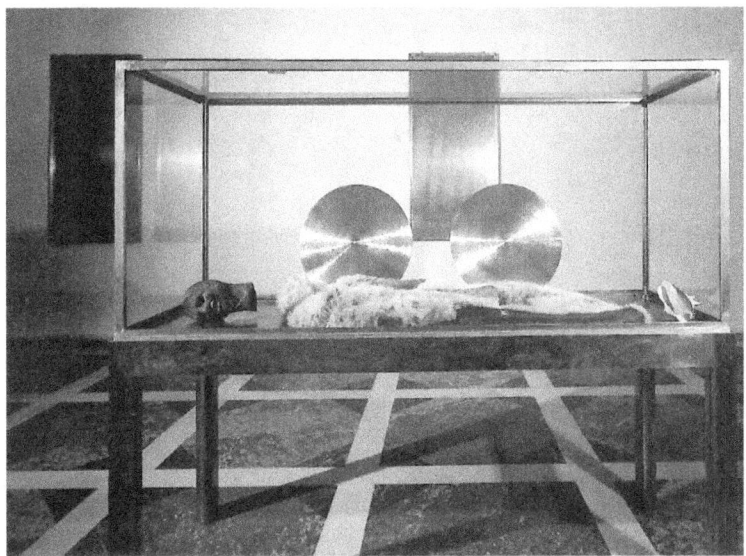

Joseph Beuys, *Palazzo Regale*, 1985. Museo di Capodimonte, Naples. Photo: Claudio Abate. © 2012 Artists Rights Society (ARS), New York / VG Bild-Kunst, Bonn

the king and his fool, are but one of the bicephalic avatars of the art-ist. There are many others of them that also show, on the one hand, his indefatigable proselytism, his political combativeness, his peda-gogical joy, his revolutionary or evolutionary optimism, his propen-sity to take the role of leader; and, on the other hand, his mystical archaism, his high sense of the pathetic in constant oscillation be-tween farce and tragedy, his tendency to play the victim, his empa-thy for all the anomic and sacrificial figures of humanity. That of Christ—victim and redeemer—is at the crossing of a double series of identifications: chief and child, priest and scapegoat, shepherd and coyote, stag and hare, composer and thalidomide baby, social reformer and rebel, legislator and outlaw, statesman and prisoner, mediator and recluse, orator and deaf-mute, prophet and buffoon, professor and student, shaman and sham, utopianist of the future and embalmer of the past.

The ritual, obsessive, and quasi-exhaustive character of this list of the roles Beuys incarnated (lacking—and this is significant—only that of worker and prostitute) sets up echoes between his work and

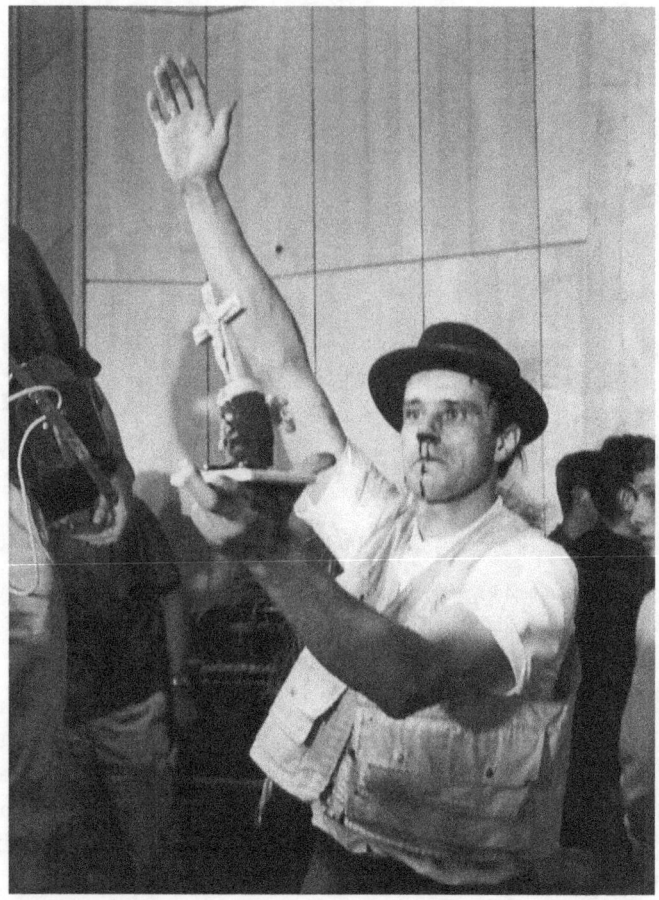

Joseph Beuys, *Beuys-Christ*—Joseph Beuys after having been hit on the nose by a protester during his action *Kukei, akopee-Nein!*, Braunkreuz, Fettecken, Modellfettecken, Festival der Neuen Kunst, Technische Hochschule, Aachen, 20 July 1964. © 2012 Artists Rights Society (ARS), New York / VG Bild-Kunst, Bonn

an already extensive litany of similar identifications, all of them allegorical of the condition of the artist within modernity, all of them leading directly—more than a century distant—to a mythical country peopled with all the romantic figures of the excluded as bearers of social truth. The name of this country—where *flâneurs* and dandies cross paths with peddlers and ragpickers; where *rapins* and *carabins* (would-be painters and medical students) thumb their noses at philistines; where the sins of the streetwalker are redeemed by the love of a young poet; where humanity is more humane in the brothel than in the church or palace; where the underworld is the true aristocracy, tuberculosis the pardon for syphilis, and talent the only riches—the name of this country that rings with all the cries of injustice and where the only one radically denied a visa is the bourgeois, that name is of course *bohemia*. It is a literary and imaginary country where, in a deformed image at once tragic and ideal, there was dreamed a humanity to replace the real humankind that peopled nineteenth-century Europe, and that industrial capitalism had pitilessly set against itself by dividing it into two new antagonistic classes, the bourgeoisie and the proletariat. The real name of bohemia, or, better, the name of its correlate in the actual world, is the *Lumpenproletariat*: a no-man's-land into which there fell a certain number of people incapable of finding a place within the new social divisions—expropriated farmers, out-of-work craftsmen, penniless aristocrats, country girls forced into prostitution. Dickens and Zola have described this dark fringe of industrialization, these shady interstices of urbanization. Like Baudelaire, Hugo, and many other novelists who, unlike them, did not profess naturalism, they drew their inspiration from this marginal society, but they also contributed to the fabrication of its image, its transposition into bohemia. The *Lumpenproletariat* functions all the more as the figure of a humanity of replacement in that it is a suffering humanity, in that only in its midst do the true human values of liberty, justice, and compassion survive, and in that it harbingers a promise of reconciliation. To the denizens of bohemia, Daumier, Degas, Toulouse-Lautrec, the Picasso of the Rose and Blue Periods, Rouault, and many others gave the faces of Don Quixote and Scapin, of laundresses and opera dancers, of dwarfs and nightclub singers, of circus artists and harlequins, the face of Mary Magdalene and that of Christ.

It is to this gallery of portraits that Beuys adds his own; it is this gallery that he recapitulates and brings full circle, and that he refers—perhaps unwittingly—to its conditions of emergence. All these portraits show the artist as bohemian, incarnating both the suffering humanity of the present and the just man of the future. All are portraits of the artist as a proletarian. *The proletarian*—as translating *the bohemian* as a social type that excludes *the bour-geois* but includes all the rest of humanity suffering from industrial capitalism—is not (or not necessarily) a member of the proletariat, that is, of the working class. Of this latter, the myth of bohemia offers a displaced and transposed image; it makes of a transnational reality an imaginary country, a quasi-nation, without real territorial frontiers, peopled with nomads and gypsies, as unreal as Alfred Jarry's Poland. The worker himself is rarely an inhabitant. The image of bohemia is ideological because it occults the reality that it is precisely charged with transposing: the massive proletarization of all the men and women who did not belong to the bourgeoisie. But *the proletarian* is a construction no less ideological—or mythical— of the same personage or social type that the bohemian expresses in the discourse of art and literature. Simply, it expresses it in the discourse of political economy, that of Marx, and even more specifically, of the young Marx.

What, then, is a proletarian for Marx? He is someone—no matter who—who finds himself to have everything to lose from the capitalist regime and everything to gain from its overthrow. Everything to lose, which is to say, his very humanity; and everything to gain, this same humanity. From the beginnings of industrial capitalism on, the proletarian is a figure torn from the horizon of its own future disappearance. He is literally the prototype of the universal man of the future, the anticipated type of the free and autonomous man, the emancipated man, the man who will have fully realized his human essence. The latter lies in the fact that man is a productive, social being. Against the ground of such an ontological substrate, the history of men is then nothing but the growth of productive forces and the progress of the social relations of production. For Marx conceives of man only as *homo faber*: labor—the faculty of producing—is what makes him man, and the consciousness he has of it is the import of his humanity. It transforms simple biological belonging to the human species into consciousness of participating in humankind and thus makes of all products of labor the privileged place of collective living. This is why the social relation is the essence of the individual as *Gattungswesen* (species-being), and why, in turn, all social relations are, in the last instance, reduced to relations of production. These will be free and autonomous only with

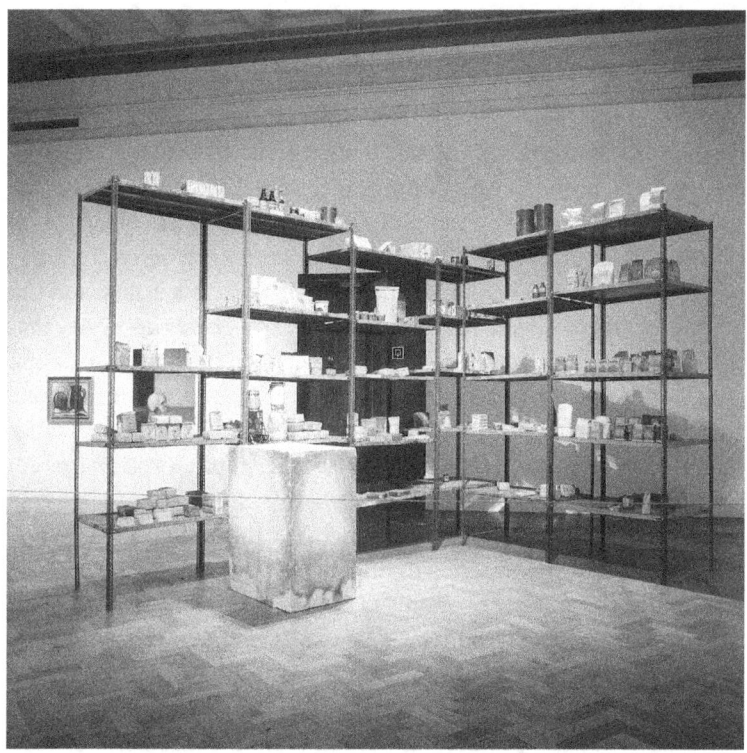

Joseph Beuys, *Wirtschaftswerte*, 1980. Photo: Phillippe De Gobert. © 2012 Artists Rights Society (ARS), New York / VG Bild-Kunst, Bonn

the advent of the class- and stateless society, the communist society of which the proletariat is the avant-garde. In the meantime class struggle will be the order of the day, since the proletariat is exploited and alienated by the capitalist regime to which it is subjected, or, to put it another way, since *the proletarian*, dispossessed of his human essence by social relations of production that admit of nothing but the regime of private property, still needs to reappropriate it through struggle.

Even while already being, in anticipation, the type or prototype of man-in-general, the proletarian suffers from being exploited and alienated under the yoke of capitalism. Exploitation, which consists in the fact that surplus value is extracted from the unpaid labor time that the worker is constrained to offer to the owner of the means of production who employs him, is a damage he suffers from, an injury that a regrouping of the working forces through unionization could lessen or repair to a certain degree. But alienation is not a damage that can be made up for; it is a wrong that must be righted. It derives from the nature of the transaction between wageworker and employer meeting in the capitalist labor market, as if each were in possession of a ware in which the other is interested, in order to proceed to their exchange. The capitalist offers a salary and the worker his labor power. Now labor power—*Arbeitskraft* or *Arbeitsvermögen*—is, par excellence, that which defines or will define man as productive and social being, universal man in his essence. To have to sell his being as if it were a belonging is precisely what alienates *homo faber* and makes the worker into a *proletarian*. All languages distinguish the verbs *to be* and *to have*; these are verbs that do not translate into one another. Yet this is what the regime of private property pretends to do where it treats labor power as a commodity, "neither more nor less than sugar," Marx says. Therein rests the irreparable wrong that Marx calls alienation and that only the abolition of private ownership of the means of production will right.

To say that the proletarian suffers from a confusion between two verbs might seem rather light in view of what the working class has had to endure. Marx is much more concrete: it's his life that the worker alienates in selling his labor power to the capitalist; it's his muscular and cerebral force that he cedes to the capitalist; his blood that he spills for the capitalist; his skin that he wears out; his flesh that he exhausts. But this loss follows from exploitation; it does not involve any alienation, any alteration of man's essence. After all, the salary that his boss pays him allows the worker to reconstitute his lost energies; it is even exactly calculated for the reproduction of his labor power to make up for the expenditure. It is true that the worker wears himself out, but like everyone else, he is subjected to the irreversible march of time. It is also true that he gives away more time—labor time, that is, sole measure of the value of the commodities he produces—than he receives back in the form of wages, but this is because he is exploited. Once again, there is no case for calling that alienation. In fact, the Hegelian concept of alienation disappears from the writings of Marx after the Manuscripts of 1844. As for that of labor power, it does not appear before 1865, in *Value, Price, and Profit*. In the first edition of *Wage-Labor and Capital*, which dates from 1849, the wageworker does not sell his labor power to the capitalist, but simply his labor. It is only in the posthumous edition of 1891, amended by Engels (who accounts for it in the preface) in order to factor in the theoretical advances of *Capital*, that labor power takes the place of labor. This replacement is hard to uphold as such without the concept of alienation, lest one see the essential protagonist of class struggle, the proletarian, vanish like a ghost. Which is why the 1865 introduction of labor power rehabilitates under the table the concept of alienation, or at least rescues its ontological and dialectical sense, which remains crucial to Marx's thinking throughout. The 1849 conception, however, was more logical and more exact: the measure of exchange-value being labor, and the measure of labor being time, it is obviously time that the capitalist treats as commodity and "measures with the clock, as he measures sugar with a scale." But once the concept of alienation is abandoned, whether it be his labor or his labor time that the wageworker sells, no wrong is done him. He suffers the injury that is exploitation, but that is reparable. A better distributive justice could render exploitation tolerable, as has effectively occurred in the Western democracies. To justify the revolution and to write the abolition of capitalism onto the political agenda, it is necessary that the wageworker suffer a wrong that affects him in his human essence. If it is his labor power that he sells, if he is forced to part with the very thing that constitutes him in his humanity, then he suffers this wrong, then he is a proletarian and not simply a salaried worker, then this wrong must be righted for him to reappropriate his humanity. (The word *appropriation* betrays the embarrassment of a Marx caught in the trap of his own thought and forced to treat the essence of *homo faber* in theory in the same manner as the capitalist treats it in practice.)

Whether its messianic import was religious, political, or cultural in coloration, an enormous part of modern art has demanded that the wrong done to the proletarian be righted—in other words, that the labor power of man-in-general (the individual as *Gattungs-wesen*) be liberated and "disalienated." Virtually all modern art utopias have claimed to unleash the productive power man has in himself, yet of which he remains dispossessed to the extent, precisely, that he can merely have it, whereas it constitutes or will constitute him in his being, in his at once unique and universal belonging to humankind. It is to this demand and to this claim that modern or avant-garde artists (those at least who fully claimed those titles) have testified, by incarnating *the proletarian*. What is at stake here has little to do with certain artists' ideological alignments with proletarian positions—this existed but remained the exception—and is not in contradiction to the objective economic situation of artists, which is more akin to that of a small entrepreneur than to that of a wageworker. Subjectively speaking, the modern artist is the proletarian par excellence, because the regime of private property forces him to place on the art market things that will be treated as commodities but that, in order to have aesthetic value, must be productions and concretions of his labor power and, if possible, of nothing else. Even while the bourgeois conception of art "reifies" the work (via the market) on the one hand, on the other, it judges the work (via the aesthetic) for the way it manifests this faculty of *producing value*, a value that, in order to be authentic, must be unique to the artist and promise to be valid for all, and thus must have its seat in the very nature of the artist as individual human-in-general.

Marx calls this universal faculty of producing value *labor power*; Beuys calls it *creativity*, and he is certainly not the first to give it this name, far from it. He is more like the last to be able to do this with conviction. Beuys's art, his discourse, his attitude, and above all the two faces presented by his persona—the suffering face and the utopian face—sing the swan song of creativity, the most powerful of the modern myths. Perched on a threshold that he called "the end of modernity," Beuys was in effect its doorman. Yet the postmodernity onto which he hoped to open the door is as black as his own death. For this tragic and optimistic Janus is above all pathetic; both his faces are turned backward, toward the modernity that he brings to a close. It could not be otherwise, since that which Beuys promised under the name of creativity is what all of artistic modernity never ceased to promise, to hope for, to invoke as the emancipatory horizon of its achievement. "Everyone is an artist." Rimbaud, Novalis already said it long ago; the students of 1968, in the streets of Paris, on California campuses, or gathered around Beuys in Düsseldorf, proclaimed it once again and wrote it on the walls. It always meant, since the German Romantics, "Power to the imagination." It has never become a reality, at least not in that sense. But all the will to emancipation and the desire for disalienation the nineteenth and twentieth centuries have carried have always meant that everyone is an artist, but the masses don't have the power to actualize this potential because they are oppressed, alienated, and exploited; only those few whom we stupidly call professional artists know that in reality their vocation is to incarnate this unactualized potential. Hence the two faces of modernity, of which it is Beuys's pathetic grandeur to have worn both: the public, revolutionary, and pedagogical face, the one that shouts that an adequate teaching will liberate the masses' creativity; and the secret, insane, and rebellious face, the one that claims that creativity is already of this world precisely where it lies fallow and in waiting, crude and savage: in the art of madmen, children, and primitives. If he had lived in the Germany of the Weimar Republic, Beuys could have been at once Gropius and Beckmann, or perhaps a Klee amended by Lehmbruck.

Clearly Marx does not slip out of the mythic fabric of modernity; he is among the most formidable of its craftsmen. Creativity is to the cultural field what labor power is to the field of political economy. The two fields imbricate throughout the course of modernity and in all possible manners. With Beuys—this is why the translation attempted here is so easy—the two fields perfectly overlap, and their overlapping is the signal that their dialectic is over. During the last decade of his life and work, Beuys constructed an actual political economy on which he hoped to found his theory of *social sculpture*. It was moored in creativity, which is more than a universal faculty of man; it is the one that makes him man. "Der Mensch ist das kreative Wesen," Beuys has said over and over again, as if echoing Marx. Like labor power, but unlike talent—a notion on which classical aesthetics is based—creativity is the potential of each and every one, and, being the capacity to produce in general, it precedes the division of

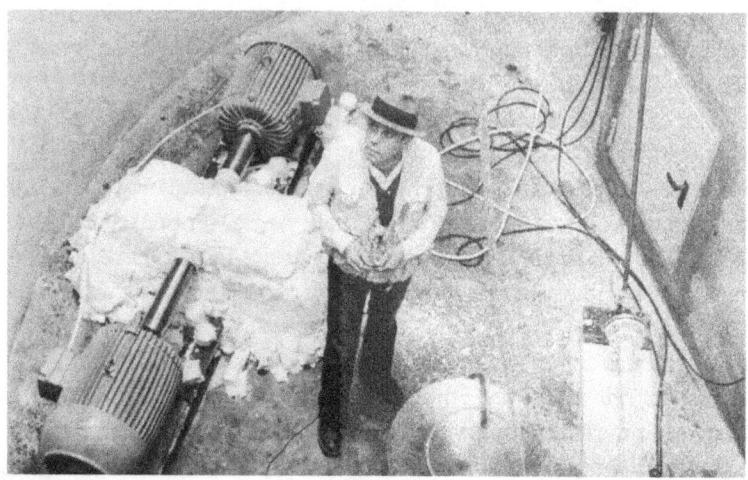

Joseph Beuys, *Honigpumpe*, 1977. Documenta 6, Kassel. © 2012 Artists Rights Society (ARS), New York / VG Bild-Kunst, Bonn

labor. From this it follows that everyone is an artist and that art is not a profession. All productive activity, whether of goods or of services, can be called art; creativity is the true capital; the exchange of goods is to the flow of creativity in the social body what the circulatory system is to the flow of vital force in the individual body. (This is what the *Honigpumpe* from the 1977 Documenta symbolized.)

In order that this utopia become reality and that creativity be "disalienated," goods, money included, must not be commodities. Money, called "production capital," would be created from scratch by a central bank (it embodies neither time nor labor power) and distributed democratically. Once placed in the hands of social agents, it would become "consumption capital," paper money with no value but that of representing a certain purchasing power, a value that it will lose in the course of the transaction before returning to the central bank and being reinjected into the economic circuit. Beuys intended in this way to neutralize private ownership of the means of production—a lovely, naive, and hardly original utopia with Fourierist and Proudhonist overtones. Marx had already denounced a similar one proposed by John Gray. It is difficult to see in it more than an involuntary caricature of numerous broken promises of modernity, a slightly grotesque farce with nothing but a retrospective meaning. The last of the proletarians has tried to right the wrong of his condition—which is that of all artists, and since everyone is an artist, of everyone—by mapping the hopes and prophecies of the modern cultural field onto the field of political economy, in order to revive them. But he has not seen that if they in fact find a part of their historical truth there, it is in the past tense, for the translations made possible by this mapping, and not in the future tense, for the emancipation it was *the proletarian*'s vocation to promise.

There remains the suffering of the proletarian and the pathetic irony implying that if the promise of emancipation should be abandoned, the personage of the proletarian would vanish. Beuys the sculptor knew how, with pain and humor alike, to work out the contradictions that Beuys the charlatan economist pretended with utter seriousness to dissolve. The talented artist didn't do the same thing as the prophet of creativity. When it is convincing, his work testifies; it promises nothing. Until further notice money, not creativity, constitutes capital; everyone has not become an artist; the art market continues to treat as commodities the productions exuded by the "creativity" of those it recognizes as professional artists. In this regard Beuys was coddled: alienated, perhaps, but not exploited.

Raum 90.000 DM, an environment produced in 1981, states its own price. Strewn over the room, five old, rusted drums, once having contained various industrial chemical products, warn of the ecological damages and wrongs wrought by industry (one of them had contained fluorocarbon, the pollutant responsible for destroying the ozone layer) and testify to the consumption of use value. Useless and used up, the drums will be treated nonetheless as precious objects by the commercial gallery that shows them, wholly aware of their exchange value. But by arranging them as unaesthetically as possible (they don't even make an interesting formal configuration), Beuys succeeds in making their presence incongruous and frustrating. They are different sizes and filled to different levels with scraps of aluminum slag that have been fused together. One of them overflows, and a ladle is attached to the mound of debris.

The staging is allegorical, and the allegory is pessimistic: under the conditions of industrial capitalism (the containers), artists' creativity (the contents) can only congeal into commodities and become alienated in their exchange value. The artist is supposed to draw from the well of his labor power, but the alchemy that turns it into gold for the dealer leaves him nothing but slag ("coagulated labortime," Marx would say).

In a corner of the room, facing this arrangement, is crammed a large copper bathtub filled to the brim with a solution of sulfuric acid. This is another allegory of the artist, and this time the well is alive. Under the conditions of a renewal (the container: the theme of the bathtub has autobiographical resonances of baptism and rebirth in Beuys's work), the creativity of artists (the contents: as corrosive as the original contents of the drums were polluting) preserves its subversive potential. But the container is itself contained; the bathtub is not bare but enveloped in a thick layer of terra cotta that seems to protect it and to hide in the depths of its material some strange pouches that the sculptor has modeled as if they were the pockets of a beggar's wallet or of the artist's famous vest. The dialectic of contained containers (of conditioning conditions) does not stop there, and even overflowing with corrosive labor power, the bathtub does not escape exchange value. Getting a jump on the dealer, Beuys gouged the price of the work into the still-damp clay: "90.000 DM." Illusion has no foothold. Time gets the last word. Beuys, who understood materials like no one else, knew that in drying the clay would contract and would end up cracking. Whether by chance or by design, one of the fissures has neatly sliced through the price and separated the nine from the zeros, symbolically canceling the monetary value of the work. The bathtub of creativity breaks out of its sheath of reification, and the artist strips off his old man's cloak, ready to bear the novices of the Beuysian utopia to the baptismal font. The ensemble is more ridiculous than sublime, and formally only semiconvincing. To the left of the bathtub, negligently pinned to the wall, a collage of notes and sketches mounted between two sheets of glass pretends to explain the work and explains nothing, as should be.

Time always has the last word indeed, and time cracks statues and corrodes utopias more surely than sulfuric acid. Creativity has nothing subversive left; that myth is dated. *Raum 90.000 DM*

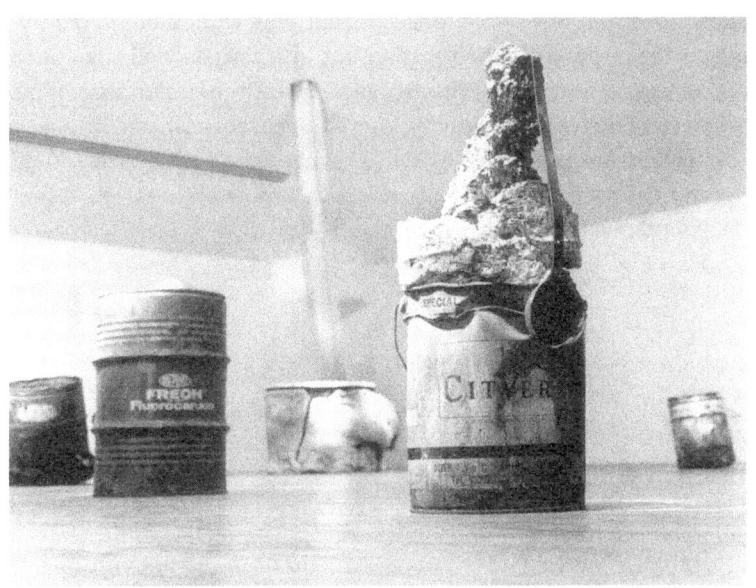

Joseph Beuys, *Raum 90 000 DM*. Photo: Jean Baptiste Rodde. © 2012 Artists Rights Society (ARS), New York / VG Bild-Kunst, Bonn

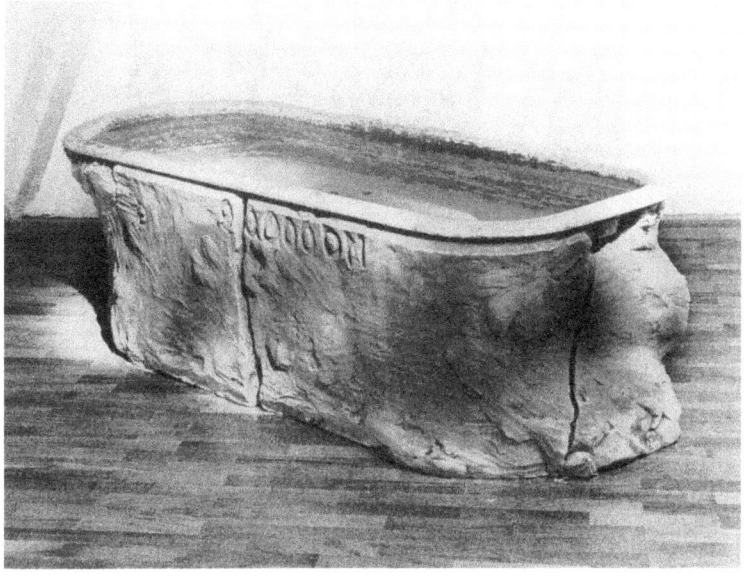

Joseph Beuys, *Raum 90 000 DM*. Photo: Jean Baptiste Rodde. © 2012 Artists Rights Society (ARS), New York / VG Bild-Kunst, Bonn

subscribes to it but also exposes its extreme vulnerability, testifying to the hope of the proletarian but attesting as well the comic aspect of this character. With Beuys gone and the concretions of his talent (and not of his creativity) more than ever fetishized by a necrophilic art market, time will decide whether his sculpture should survive the ruin of *social sculpture*, this modern *Kunstwollen* that he ignited one last time.

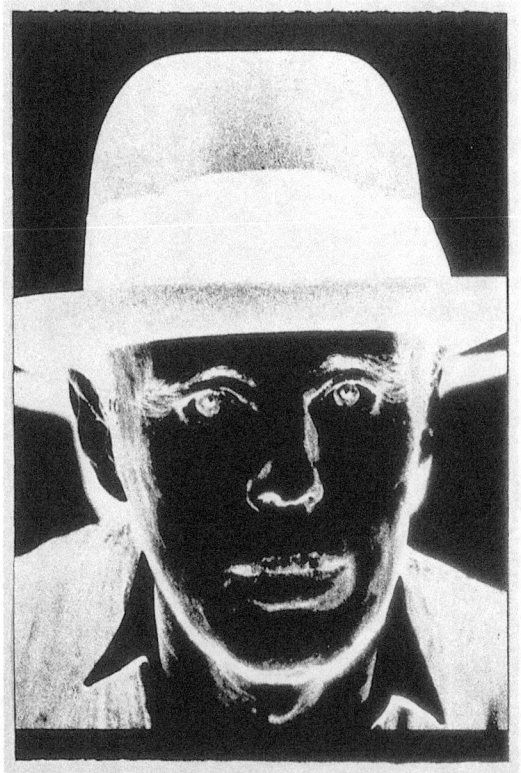

Andy Warhol, *Joseph Beuys*, 1980 Photo: The Andy Warhol Foundation, Inc. / Art Resource, NY. © 2012 The Andy Warhol Foundation for the Visual Arts, Inc. / Artists Rights Society (ARS), New York

Andy Warhol, or
The Machine Perfected

In counterpoint to Joseph Beuys one is tempted to place Andy Warhol, to oppose to the vitalism and populism of the former the *morbidezza* and worldliness of the latter. In the art of recent decades only Warhol equals Beuys in legend value—that is, media-status—and the shadows of both of them hover equally over the art of the younger generation. But Beuys is a hero and Warhol is a star. The former had to immolate himself on a stage dating from the *Comédie humaine*, and his aesthetic is theatrical, confusing art and life in the same authenticity. The life and art of the latter were projections of the same lifestyle, and his aesthetic is that of the simulacra dated by Hollywood. Beuys's art demands a myth of origin and a historical telos, that of Warhol the fiction of the eternal return and the steady state of posthistory. For one, capitalism remained the cultural horizon to leave behind; for the other, it was simply nature. Beuys, like Marx a bourgeois German, sought to incarnate the proletarian. Warhol, an American immigrant of working-class origins, wanted to be a machine. At the nexus of these oppositions are several related facts: that Beuys based art on will and thus on a principle of production, and Warhol based art on desire and thus on a principle of consumption; that Beuys believed in creativity and Warhol did not; and that for Beuys art was labor while for Warhol it was commerce.

Nevertheless, labor and commerce have this in common: the domain of these notions is that of political economy. It comes as no surprise, therefore, that Warhol, like Beuys, points to the same mythical country where the discourses of art and literature are mapped over that of political economy, namely, bohemia. The difference, however, is that Warhol stated boldly what Beuys, as a true romantic, forced us to decipher. In order to translate the *bohemian* into the *proletarian*, as is appropriate for Beuys, it was necessary to pass through Marx. Warhol did the translation himself: he called his bohemia the Factory. But it was precisely *his* bohemia, a simulacrum of bohemia, having nothing any longer to do with the literary myth whose historical raison d'être was to give a voice to the Lumpenproletariat's suffering and hope. His factory was not served by proletarians any more than the 1960s underground was peopled by masses of workers locked into the underworld of Metropolis. In the Factory one led the bohemian life, played at it, but was not subjected to it as to a fatal destiny. Drugs and sex, eccentricities, posturing as the *poète maudit* certainly took their toll, but these personal tragedies were the price to pay for a lifestyle that was beautiful only in its coherence and would not amount to a life in the full sense, the life of the species-being (*Gattungswesen*) in which Marx locates the essence of the proletarian. Unlike Marx's proletarians, whose labor power unites them as individuals both belonging to the exploited, alienated class and carrying the emancipated destiny of the species, the inhabitants of the Factory are isolated individuals. There were no social types in Warhol's bohemia, no acrobats or ragpickers, but rather proper names: Edie Sedgwick, Gerard Malanga, Ron Tavel, Brigid Polk, Candy Darling, Viva, Ondine, Billy Name . . . each with his or her look, quirks, neurosis, sexual specialty, and idiom. This world of freaks gravitated around a central figure who had himself called the boss but who made it a point of honor never to seem to have the slightest individuality, never to be anything but the mirror of his entourage, the xerox of what his courtiers wanted him to be. He managed the Factory not like a boss but like a madame, if he managed it at all.

Beuys incarnated the whole list of social types that filled bohemia—dandy, peddler, medical student, poet—except for two: the worker and the whore. The worker, or rather the proletarian, supplies the key to a reading of this list, causing it to reverberate one last time in all the modern utopias that sought to liberate creativity in order to fulfill human needs and to render art its use value. Warhol, who perhaps believed in divine providence but surely not

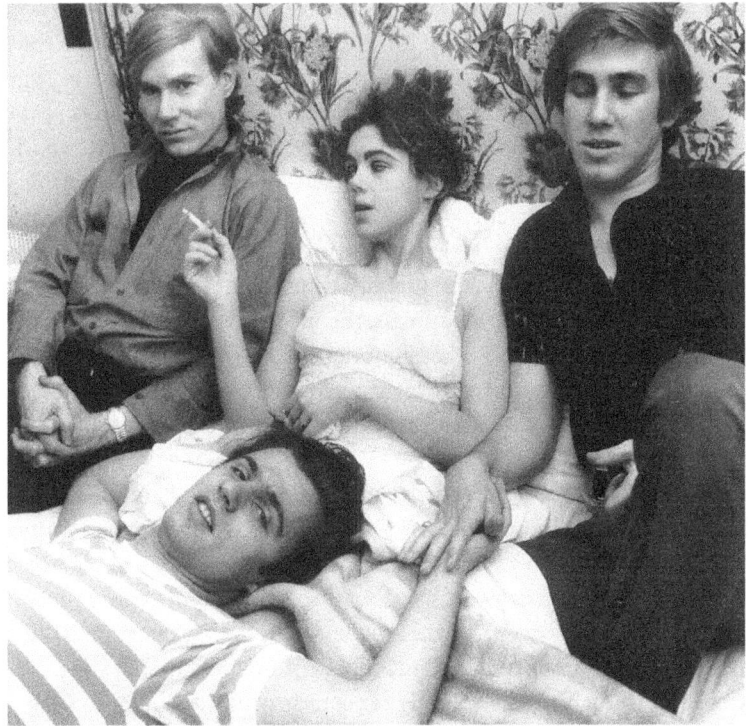

Andy Warhol, Edie Sedgwick, Chuck Wein, Gerard Malanga, Paris, May 1965. Photo: Shunk-Kender. © Roy Lichtenstein Foundation

in *need*, was content to base his art on the universal law of exchange by making himself the broker of the least avowable desires of his contemporaries. Warhol interpreted Beuys's equation "creativity = capital" in reverse, as had Marx when he assumed the capitalist's point of view and wrote in the 1844 manuscripts: "Through its mediating role, money is the true creative force." Warhol never made a mystery of his ambitions, nor hid the fact that he loved to swim in the "icy waters of egotistic calculation." Never did he preach utopia or promise emancipation. His philosophy (*From A to B and Back Again*) turns on the sentence "I started out as a commercial artist and I want to end up as a business artist." Which is what he did, yet not without having slipped in a dazzling and prolific career as artist between his career in the 1950s as an advertising illustrator and his career in the 1970s as a go-between in the culture industry. But *career* is the wrong word for Warhol the artist, suggesting that the fame he sought and attained also explains and justifies the great artist he was, at least between 1961 and 1968. Not only does fame explain nothing of the kind, but coming from the man who prophesied, "In the future everyone will be world famous for fifteen minutes," the desire to become famous has something suspicious about it. To desire fame—not the glory of the hero but the glamour of the star—with the intensity and lucidity that Warhol did is to desire to be nothing, nothing of the human, the interior, the profound, nothing but image, surface, a bit of light on a screen, a mirror for the fantasies and a magnet for the desires of others—a thing of absolute narcissism. And to desire to outlive these desires as a *thing*, that is, not to be consumed.

In 1968 Warhol survived the violent desire of Valerie Solanas, who fired several gunshots into him. His subsequent work would suffer from this, but unlike Beuys's oeuvre, which (except his most formal objects, his drawings and watercolors) seems by no means certain to age very well, Warhol's work from the '60s improves with the passing of time. This is all the more astonishing in that it is practically nothing but a ceaselessly repeated accumulation of ordinary consumer goods: cans of Campbell's soup and boxes of Brillo pads, Coca-Cola bottles, images of stars—objects, in short, with little desirability unless viewed through the eyes of the son of Czech immigrants who grew up in poverty and for whom the egalitarianism of consumption was the very stuff of the American dream. ("The President drinks Coke, Liz Taylor drinks Coke, and, can you imagine, you can drink Coke, too.")

The American dream is a weak utopia in comparison with that of emancipation. It denies that capitalism does anyone a wrong, for it places everyone, workers and bosses, on the side of the divide where everything is already exchange value, where man's being is reckoned in belongings, where it is fair and normal that labor be treated as commodity. This is the cynicism of capital interiorized even by those it causes to suffer; this is the pleasure of the prostitute. The naiveté with which Warhol embraced the American dream finds its equal only in Beuys's economic paradise. But just as this meant that Beuys had to incarnate the proletarian, Warhol had to embody this cynical utopia. His flaunted opportunism hides a destiny that is no less tragic, not because the American dream failed but because it never stops succeeding—even where it produces as much misery as wealth. And if it succeeds, then it tolls the knell of what all pre-modern—that is, religious, artisanal, and aristocratic—civilizations have called art, and heralds the absorption of all works of art into commodities, of all aesthetic values into exchange value.

When Warhol's work is convincing, it does what Beuys's does: it promises nothing; it testifies. The American dream can of course do without promises; it needs to be real only for those who know how to get ahead. It might seem that Warhol's work is content to expose it and strip its cynicism bare. The yuppies who collect it obviously understand it this way and take pleasure in it accordingly. The left-ist criticism that castigates it precisely for not promising a beyond to the commodity understands it the same way. But to testify is nei-ther to promise nor simply to expose; it is to attest to reality as it is. It is also to reopen the possibilities of interpreting reality and forc-ing a retranslation; it is, in Warhol's case, to test the possibility of an art condition "below" or "before" the commodity. The field where this unfolds is, as with Beuys, that of political economy, and the text we must retranslate—not into the myth of emancipation but into its antithesis, the American dream—is, as always, Marx's.

What, then, are commodities for Marx? They are both artifacts—man-made products—and goods: wares possessed by *a* man. As artifacts they are the fruit of someone's labor, as goods they allow someone (else) the enjoyment of this fruit. Under these two aspects wares possess use value: the use (wear and tear) of the labor power spent for their production; the use (employment and enjoyment) of this same labor power in their consumption. But it is the entry of artifacts and goods into the circuit of exchange that makes com-modities of them. Anything whatever becomes a commodity once the use of the labor power invested in it is postponed in order that it be traded against another thing into which an equal amount of labor power has been invested, money serving as general means of equivalency. It is in this way that commodities acquire their mystical character, full of "metaphysical and theological capers," which Marx identified as fetishism. Moving, as with Beuys, between the texts of the young "romantic" Marx and those of the mature "scientific" Marx, one easily sees that in the theory of commodity fetishism (which appears in book 1 of *Capital*), the wrong caused to the producers (to the proletarians) by alienation reappears as the wrong caused to the consumers by reification.

The concept of reification (*Verdinglichung*), given pride of place by Hegelianizing Marxism (Lukács's in particular), dominates most interpretations of the passage on commodity fetishism, even though it doesn't occur there. It belongs to the same family as the Hegelian concept of alienation. Now, in *Capital*, the concept of alienation is gone, while its concrete meaning is in fact surreptitiously rehabilitated through that of use value, which now carries the sense of the *same* that must be postulated in order that a becoming-*other* be tied to it. In Marx's early writings, use value had not yet appeared. (Even in the *Grundrisse* Marx still simply speaks of "product" and attributes no *value* to it.) Between the Parisian manuscripts and *Capital*, the *Critique of Political Economy* (1859) is a pivot, for it is there that Marx vigorously introduces the two aspects under which all commodities present themselves—the couple use value and exchange value—though he still has recourse to alienation to conceptualize what will later become the theory of fetishism. But this time it is from Stuart, not from Hegel, that he borrows the concept of alienation (as well as use value, moreover), which loses its dialectical import of negation of the *same* in order to signify, on the contrary, the universal equivalence that the commodity-form imprints on the products of the concrete labor of individual workers. If for the young Marx alienation severs man from nature and his fellow men, it is because the worker alienates himself in an act of production that from the outset belongs to another, with the consequence that the product incorporating his labor faces him as a strange and lifeless object in which he cannot recognize himself. For the later Marx, alienation still severs man from nature and his fellow men, but this is now because the commodity-form valorizes in every product its exchangeability, measured by the labor time it incorporates, no matter whose labor or what its nature. For the early Marx, commodities were "objectified labor" (*vergegenständlichte Arbeit*), which nonetheless remained the particular labor of a particular man, even though in an alienated condition. For the later Marx, commodities appear as reified relations of production (*verding-*

lichte Produktionsbeziehungen), that is, as social relations between things. *Vergegenständlichung* affects the producer, having to sell himself on the labor market; *Verdinglichung* affects the consumer as well, buying for his use (his pleasure) the usage (wear and tear) of another man's labor power, as if it were in the nature of things that the most diverse labors should be commensurate, whereas it is only the nature of the market economy that renders them commensurate through exchange. The mysterious fetishism of the commodity, its hieroglyphic character (as Marx calls it), depends on the truth that the commodity reveals in the very act of hiding it, and which it hides precisely because it reveals it: the nature of the relations of production of the market economy is indeed in the nature of things, literally, since it is these very relations of production that the commodity reifies, "thingifies."

That is the truth, but it is not fair. A wrong is done to the consumers, because their pleasure in what they consume is never gained from the service the product renders but from the service that has been rendered to the product from the fact that consumption of its use value has been postponed in favor of its exchange. The capitalist who decides to produce a given commodity doesn't do so in relation to its direct utility but in relation to its expected demand on the market, and thus in relation to the exchange value of a potential use about which he cares neither whether it is actualized nor whether it responds to a real need. In the last analysis the consumer never consumes; he contributes to the turnover of the exchange value but never realizes the use value. Not only is money the perfected form of the commodity, but in a completely developed market economy—paradoxically termed consumer society—all commodities act like money. (Hence the well-known fact of consumer society: all the pleasure resides in the act of buying.) The wrong is there, and a wrong as essential to Marxist thought as that which the proletarian suffers (at any rate, it is the same one, seen from the consumer's angle), which must be righted. Yet once the Hegelian concept of alienation is abandoned, it can be righted only if resting on the postulate that use value has ontological existence. If Marx did not postulate the reality of needs, if he did not hold that use value always has a natural substratum or that the labor creating use value is independent of all social forms, in short, if he had not held above

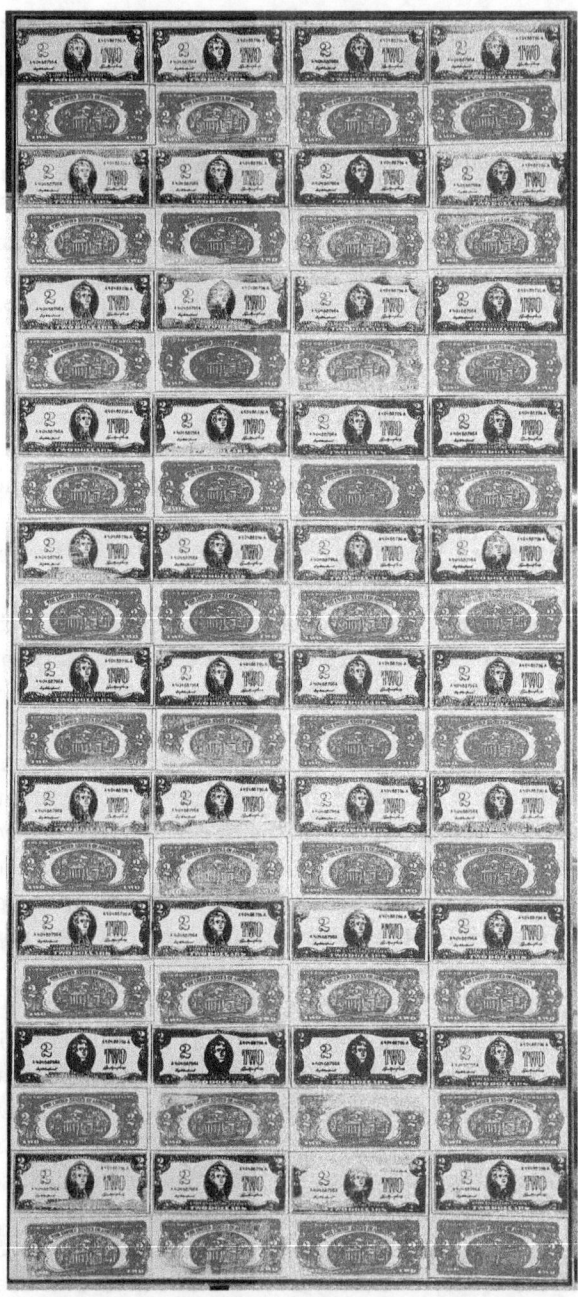

Andy Warhol, *80 Two Dollar Bills (Front and Rear)*, 1962. Collection Musée national d'art moderne, Paris. © 2012 The Andy Warhol Foundation for the Visual Arts, Inc. / Artists Rights Society (ARS), New York

all that utility is a value, even the true value, the only one that humanizes economic production, then the horizon of a communist society—where things will manifest social relations worthy of the name between men, rather than men, all dealing in exchange, manifesting social relations between things—this horizon would vanish.

Much of modern art demanded that the wrong done to consumers be righted. This presupposed that the public for art (not only its buyers) be understood, consciously or not, as a public of consumers and that aesthetic pleasure be perceived as an act of consumption. Now, only use value can be consumed; but under capitalism, use value is nothing but an advance taken on exchange. Exchange value is the only *value*, as Marx was forced to recognize in more than one place. From this derive the three paths modern artists have explored in order to resist the domination of exchange value. The first path was trod by those artists who attempted to put their practice in the service of utilitarianism—whether social, economic, or political—and who tied their fate to the perspective of an overcoming of capitalism. It is the path of Russian productivism and of functionalism, as at Hannes Meyer's Bauhaus, for example: industrial design, agitprop, realism, and *Sachlichkeit* all hold that aesthetic values are use values. The second path relies on the fact that the art market is only imperfectly a market and in many respects is a carryover of precapitalist relations of production. The artists who took that path attempted to push the old aesthetic of contemplation to its most extreme consequences (abstraction, suprematism, the monochrome as a form of the sublime, etc.) and to retain from use value its value (*wealth*, as economists before Marx called it), entirely denying its utility: aesthetic contemplation is held to be disinterested and to consume nothing. Finally, the artists taking the third path attempted to do the opposite and retain from use value the use and not the value: the work of art is to manifest its wear, and the artistic act its destruction, as pure loss. An aesthetic of ostentatious consumption exempts the public from consuming and calls on an economy of expenditure (*dépense*) or of gift and counter-gift, which neither the liberal nor the Marxist economy had foreseen. Bataille theorized it in *La part maudite*, and Dubuffet, the *affichistes*, Tinguely, Vostell, and the art of happenings provide some examples.

Warhol belongs to none of these three traditions. He does not demand that a wrong be righted, nor does he fight against the metamorphosis of art lovers into consumers. On the contrary, he positions them as such, as explicitly as possible. In confronting them with rows of Campbell's soup cans, he registers what in any case they have already become. They are consumers, and the painting is a commodity. Yet Warhol testifies to this situation; he is not content with registering it like a mirror as cynical as the reflection it returns. If it is the case that in art the whole of modernity tied its hopes to the myths of creativity, disalienation, dereification, then Warhol is not modern. But was Matisse modern—he who wanted his painting to be an armchair for the tired businessman? Are aesthetic values sustained by the power of the myths that nourished them, myths that have failed? They are not *values*: such is the answer Warhol implies, one of whose famous sayings was "I want to be Matisse," and another, no less famous, "I want to be a machine"—two desires whose conjunction, though surprising, ought to be taken seriously. The first shows the ambition concealed behind the quip about the "business artist," and the second is not a quip.

Fair or unfair, it is a fact that the art market, to the precise degree that it is a market, treats works of art as commodities and absorbs aesthetic values into the sole exchange value. But that is true, or relevant, only if the aesthetic field is totally mapped onto the field of political economy (this mapping that the later Beuys incarnated)— in other words, if aesthetics has to do with values. It is not true if works of art incorporate no value, no exchange value. One doesn't leave the field of political economy—quite the contrary. Like Beuys, and even more explicitly, Warhol maps it totally onto the aesthetic field, like the Borgesian map that is congruent with the territory it represents. But Warhol seems to hold out a fourth possibility, one apparently unexplored by the modernists, in order to make art signify that the judgment which names it as such has no more to do with value than it had to do with piety in those days when the aesthetic field was entirely mapped onto the religious field. This path gives up emancipation and has no faith in creativity; it does not claim to right a wrong, since it perceives none; it ignores use value and recognizes only exchange value; it instantiates art not in will but in desire, and a very peculiar one: to be a machine.

Machines, according to good political economy, Marxist or not, are constant capital. They don't work, they don't produce value.

The only source of value is human labor, and its only measure, labor time. It is as though Warhol also had his own brand of utopia, a weak utopia streamlined by the American dream, the dream of a society which automation would rid of the working class, and where everyone would be a consumer, no one a producer. In the Factory, even if Warhol had himself called the boss, he still wasn't Vasarely. He didn't buy machines to increase his productivity and flood the world with silkscreens; he *was* the machine, or at least said he wanted to be one. Sure, this was wishful thinking. Psychologically speaking, it certainly meant to Warhol the desire to be without desire, to be insentient, to be beyond suffering or the fear of death. And all his work shows, often in a most moving fashion, that this desire was merely a desire. But economically speaking, to want to be a machine means to maintain that artists don't work. Not that Warhol worked less than anyone else. Simply, the labor time that an artist puts into his work is not relevant, because it is not on the same order as the average, socially necessary labor time (as Marx calls it) that constitutes the substance of exchange value. All artists are machines in this sense. And just as Beuys was not the first artist to want to incarnate the proletarian, Warhol was not the first to wish to be a machine.

Ever since Delaroche, Champfleury, and Baudelaire expressed the fear, inspired in them by photography, of seeing the painter replaced by a machine, modern painters—the great ones, those who deserve to be called avant-garde—have responded with an expression of their desire to be one. Courbet, who professed that "nothing that imprints itself on the retina is outside the domain of painting," was the first to give a strictly photographic definition for it. Manet, who simplified chiaroscuro and succeeded in seizing the blank amazement of his models as if struck by a magnesium flash, gave the canvas a passionate indifference that had its equal only in the passivity of the automated image. Monet, as if he were outracing photography's speed, recorded in his Rouen cathedrals and his haystacks the light of the instant as it hit and imprinted the canvas. Seurat, in a development contemporary with the invention of the autochrome by the Lumière brothers, digitized the palette and mechanized the hand. Cézanne, who admired Monet for being "nothing but an eye" and Courbet for not knowing what he painted even though he produced the most exact likeness of it, also spelled out, literally, what the driving desire of all painting since realism and impressionism had been, by upholding that "the free brain of the artist should be like a photographic plate, a simple recording device, when he is working." Warhol's desire has been explicit ever since, as has been the fact that it is not just any machine that painters wished to be, but precisely the one that put their craft and their economic survival in jeopardy. From Mondrian to Ryman, from Léger to Lichtenstein, from Moholy-Nagy to Stella, contempt for the hand, the desire to give the surface as standardized a texture as possible, the pleasure drawn from repetition, have all displayed the surprising wish that the body of the artist at work be segmented, Taylorized, mechanized, like that of the worker of *Modern Times*, but in order to *be* the machine and not its slave; nor, for that matter, its master. The recourse to automatism in Pollock or Borduas transfers this wish to the unconscious; the motif of the reproduction in Johns or Rauschenberg refers it to the culture of the museum without walls (*musée imaginaire*). Gerhard Richter's declaration to the effect that he does not use photography as a medium for painting, but painting as a medium for photography, summarizes the desire of the best painters throughout modernity and gives it its retrospective meaning: they reacted to the challenge of industrialization with paradoxical resistance. They could have become photographers and suffered the consequences of a new social and technical division of labor—and that's what many did, not without multiplying the contradictions tied to their ambition as artists. They could have ignored the new division of labor and painted as if the commodity-form did not affect their craft—and that is what the academic painters did, not without succumbing ever more surely to the merchandising of their work. Instead they became, in desire and in practice, not the photographer but his instrument, and even more precisely, less the camera (since for a long time it had been an instrument of painters) than the photosensitive plate, the film that records light and captures the gaze.

"If you want to know all about Andy Warhol, just look at the surface of my paintings and films and me, and there I am. There's nothing behind it." Between the producer and his production, no difference. All are commodities, fetish surfaces, and what surface has been more fetishized than photography's! Its invention threatened painters more directly than other machines other artists. Technically, it supplanted them. Economically, it threw them into an absurd race for productivity where they were beaten in advance. A progressive autonomization of the painting market—which existed before, but as part of a larger market where a social demand for images was registered, to which etchers, draftsmen, and other artisans could also respond—was the painters' and their dealers' economic response to this threat. First the market for painting separated from that of images at large, then the market of modern painting, then of a particular modernism, and of a particular artist. Each name became a little monopoly. In a monopoly situation, the price of a commodity is not determined by its exchange value; only supply and demand operate, which is why the market for living art is often assimilated to that for precious objects and antiques. But that doesn't stop painting from being treated as a commodity, with its fatal consequence the fetishization of the "handmade."

It is this fetishization that the best modern painters challenged, they who acted—and here one finds the sign of their cultural ambition—*as if* they were in fact in competition with photographers in the same general market for images, and left in their work the marks of a desire to behave *as if* their hand, their eye, their whole body were a machine for the recording and duplicating of images. Thus there are two reasons rendering "the average labor-time socially necessary" (Marx) for the production of painting-by-hand irrelevant. The plainly economic reason is that in its particular market, painting has a price but no value; the aesthetic reason, obtaining when the field of aesthetics is completely mapped onto that of political economy, is that the hand that paints behaves as though it were a sentient machine, and since machines don't labor, the picture is not a commodity. To abide by the first reason without further ado defines academic painters: they adjust supply to demand, accept that their touch is fetishized, and see to it that a price gets attached to their name. To take the second reason critically into account characterizes avant-garde or modernist painters: they start from supply and ignore demand, and attach a price to aesthetic quality alone. Above all, they challenge the fetishism of the "handmade" by asking that the object be read in terms of the social relations of production it

indeed "reifies." In other words, they treat the division of labor between painters and photographers as a cultural question their work
reflects on rather than an economic fact.

As a commercial artist, Warhol worked and drew for the advertising industry, where social demand is motivated only by the pros-
pect of exchange value, where return on investment dominates, and
where photography is used because it increases productivity. There
he practiced a craft full of outmoded charm, recognized by the profession for its very personal qualities but sold at its exchange value.
For I. Miller Shoes he drew footwear whose fetishistic connotations
(in the Freudian sense now) escaped no one and whose "handmade"
quality was underscored. Then he realized, opportunistically, that
there was more money to be made in the painting market than in advertising. It was during the heyday of abstract expressionism, when
the "handmade" was particularly prized. He was surprised that despite his many attempts no art gallery wanted his work. It had value

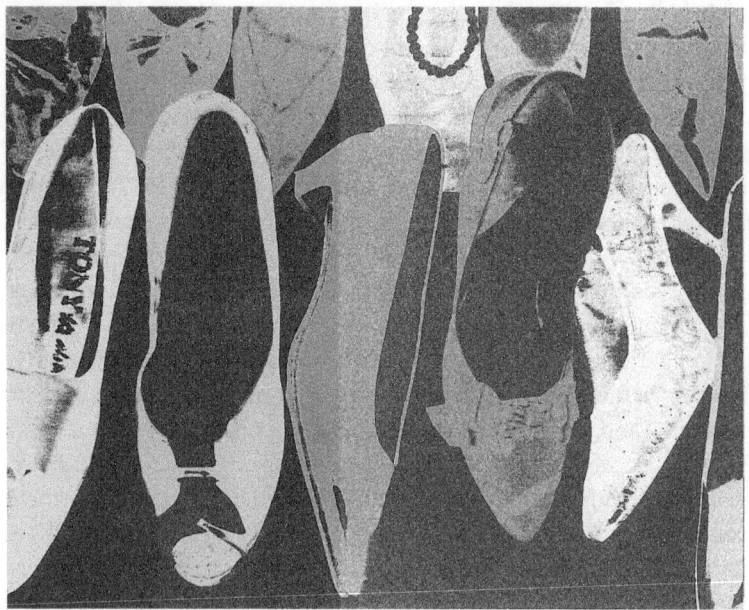

Andy Warhol, *Diamond Dust Shoes*, 1980. Photo: The Andy Warhol Foundation, Inc. /
Art Resource, NY. © 2012 The Andy Warhol Foundation for the Visual Arts, Inc. /
Artists Rights Society (ARS), New York

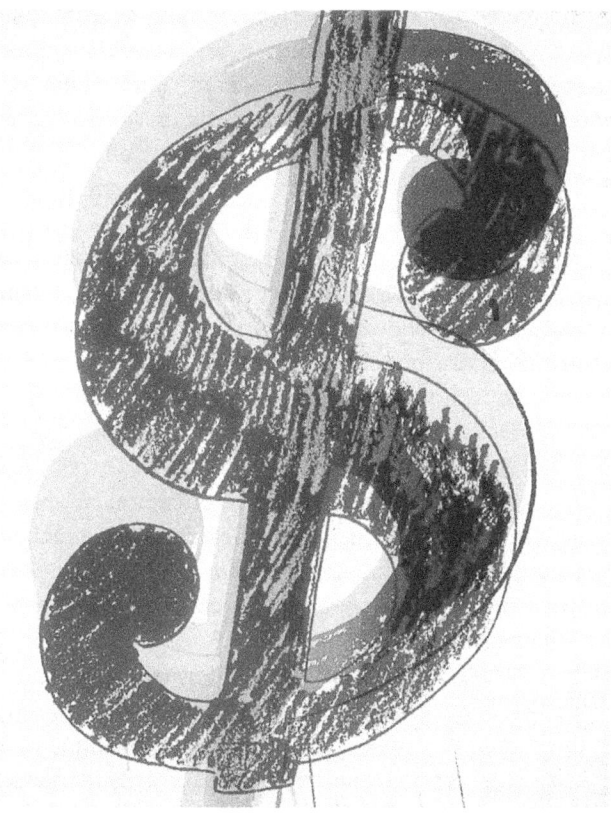

Andy Warhol, *Dollar Sign*, 1981. Photo: The Andy Warhol Foundation, Inc. / Art Resource, NY. © 2012 The Andy Warhol Foundation for the Visual Arts, Inc. / Artists Rights Society (ARS), New York

but no price. So he proceeded to show this by shifting his work to another market and by taking, realistically, exchange value as its subject matter. He proffered images of commodities, reduplicated ordinary consumer goods, made of his signature a brand name, and success came.

Warhol is the machine perfected. Not that his wish to be as numb as a machine was fulfilled. However he might have tried to appear as one, he was no less human than anyone else. Not that his work showed any less than Manet's the marks of a desire that, in order to make itself visible as desire, had to remain unsatisfied. To be the machine perfected is not to be a perfect machine. Warhol knew how to exploit the imperfections of the photo-silkscreen, the blurs, the variations of inking, the "surface incidents" (as he himself said). The more he repeated identical images, the more their accumulation made differences between them apparent and underscored their individuality. What Warhol perfected or accomplished is the historical necessity for the painter to want to be a machine. He terminated it, as Beuys terminated the historical necessity to want to incarnate the proletarian. One century after Manet, but like him and like Matisse, Warhol followed the fourth path, the one that never feared the market, the one that left it to the Don Quixotes of utopia to get upset about the transformation of art lovers into consumers or to fight against exchange value in the name of use value. With a flippancy that could shock only those who still hope that the future of the avant-gardes will be the abolition of capitalism, he did not even consider that such a struggle had meaning. He made the fetishism of commodities his philosophy, *From Andy to Baudelaire and Back Again*: from the shoes he drew with consummate charm when he was a commercial artist to the *Dollar Signs* he complacently supplied to Leo Castelli to satisfy demand after having become "business artist." With the greatest apparent cynicism he printed paper money, the commodity of all commodities, the absolute fetish. And while it was mere Monopoly money on the currency markets, it was gold on the art market. He knew the price of that which has no value. He knew how to behave not only as a painting machine but also as a filming machine, a printing machine, a recording machine, and the cash register of the art market. He perfected the modern desire to be a machine in displaying its retrospective meaning and in making explicit that the perfect mapping of the aesthetic field onto the field of political economy coincides with monopoly capitalism. The art market is a market of monopolies, far less because it is a holdover from another age, as is the market for precious objects, than because it is the specialized outlet of a culture industry that looks for monopolies anywhere it can. From then on, and all utopias aside (since neither Manet nor Matisse nor Monet nor Cézanne indulged in utopian dreams), there is no difference between the avant-garde and academicism. It's just a matter of dividing up the markets and, since monopolies never last, a simple matter of speed. Whether the

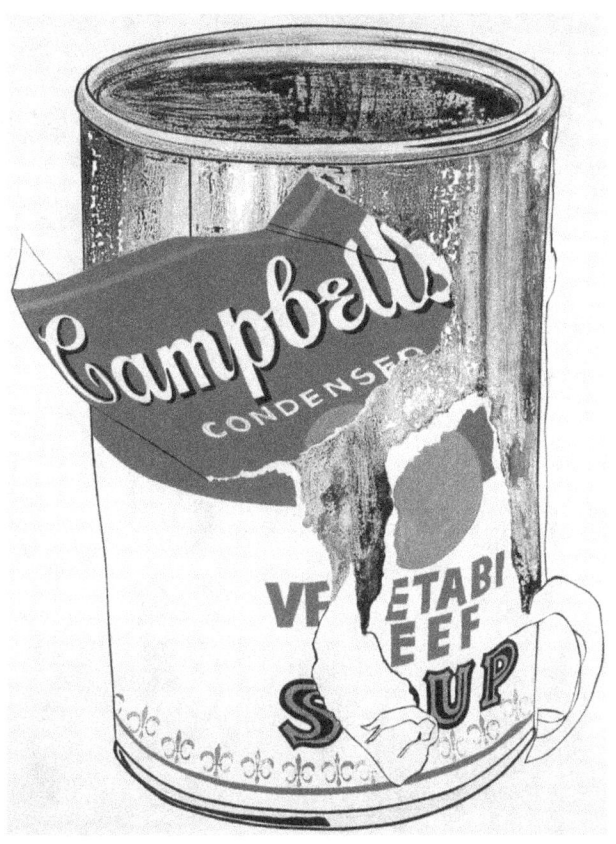

Andy Warhol, *Big Torn Campbell's Soup Can* (*Vegetable Beef*), 1962. Kunsthaus Zurich. © 2012 The Andy Warhol Foundation for the Visual Arts, Inc. / Artists Rights Society (ARS), New York

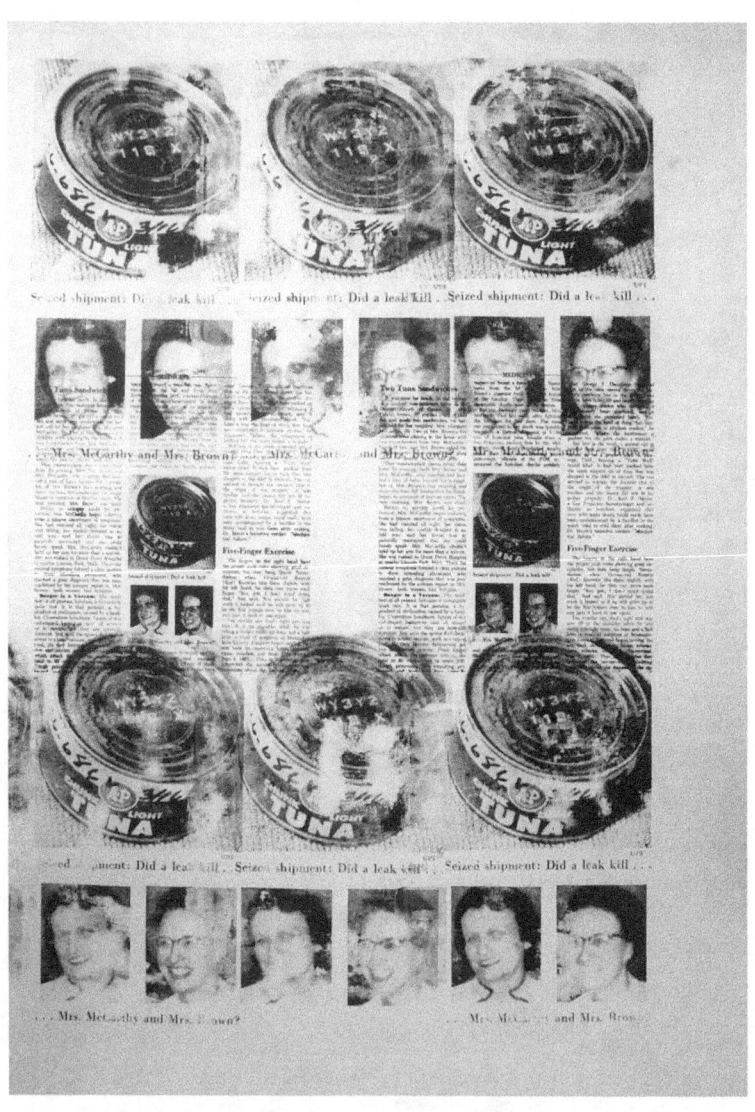

Andy Warhol, *Tunafish Disaster*, 1963. © 2012 The Andy Warhol Foundation for the Visual Arts, Inc. / Artists Rights Society (ARS), New York

name of a painter is the fetishized signature of his hand or a silk-screened brand name, as with fashion designers the *label* is what warrants the exchange value. Fifteen minutes of world fame, then disappearance into obsolescence and death.

Warhol was asked if he wanted to be a great artist, and he replied, "No, I'd rather be famous." Could it be that wanting to be famous, wanting to be a machine, and wanting to be Matisse are one and the same thing? What is most astonishing is that Warhol's work, the best of his work at any rate, that which dates from the first Factory, from before the assassination attempt by Valerie Solanas, is here to last. Perhaps this is so because he incarnated the American dream to a nightmare pitch and made visible the terrible death drive that prompts the ceaseless turnover of commodities. One doesn't take on the existence of a *thing* of absolute narcissism without drawing *jouissance* out of that which drove Marilyn to suicide. Warhol didn't evolve in the plastic world of stars so much as in the netherworld of vamps. His cinema plays out the bland dreams of 1950s Hollywood only to materialize the terror that the Hollywood of the 1920s still knew how to signal. One doesn't take on the existence of the perfected machine, one doesn't turn into a camera or a tape recorder, without also taking on the existence of all machines, and above all those that kill: the electric chair and the graves-on-wheels of the *Car Crashes*. One doesn't take on the making of one's self-portrait as a can of Campbell's soup without also putting oneself in the tins of contaminated tuna of *Tuna Fish Disaster*. Perhaps in order for the work to last, the man had to die. According to the noncausal logic of "surface incidents," he had to survive Valerie Solanas's pistol shots *because* that very day the front page of the newspapers was taken up by Robert Kennedy's assassination. The same logic decreed that he die on February 22, 1987, almost by accident, like a commodity whose defect had been detected too late.

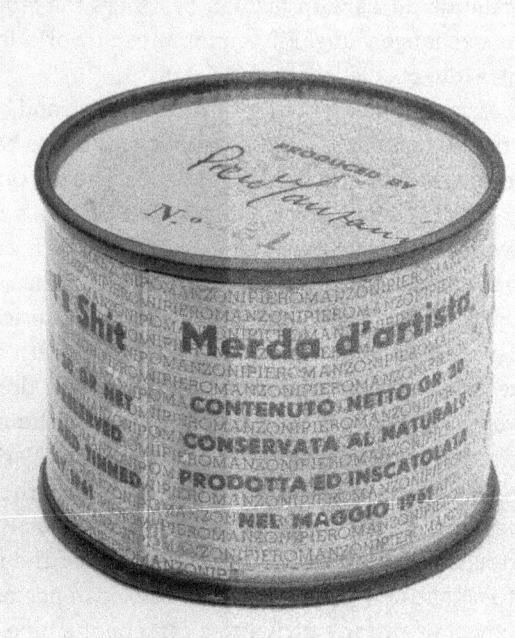

Piero Manzoni, *Merde d'artiste*, 1961. Photo: CNAC/MNAM/Dist. Réunion des Musées Nationaux / Art Resource, NY. © 2012 Artists Rights Society (ARS), New York / SIAE, Rome

Yves Klein, or The Dead Dealer

Yves Klein died on June 6, 1962, of a heart attack. It wasn't his first. Several months before, feeling that his end was near, he had ceremoniously rewritten his will in the presence of his friends, among whom were Arman and Claude Pascal—in whose company, so goes the legend, his career had begun in 1948 with a divvying up of the world. It was to them that he left *immaterial space* as well as the right to make works with *IKB* (*International Klein Blue*) and to sign his name to them. Two years earlier, he had already staged his burial in a work titled *Here Lies Space*, a *Monogold* lying flat and decorated as a tombstone with a bunch of white roses and a sponge wreath soaked with the famous blue. He had himself photographed lying beneath it.

Just as Joseph Beuys had delivered his tragic testament with *Palazzo Regale*, so does Klein with *Here Lies Space*. But it's the differences that leap to view. Beuys's double tomb was both royal and wretched, a dramatization of last rites for the *bohemian*, a vanishing historical type that the artist understood himself as embodying. With a bad taste that one suspects was calculated, Klein's tomb is that of a *petit-bourgeois gentilhomme*, and it is his alone. At the time of its conception the artist had no premonition of his coming death. The work is at once the exorcism of a rather general anxiety—a nose thumbed at the Grim Reaper—and the preparation of a publicity stunt with his coming exhibition in Krefeld in mind. It was to produce the nifty effect of showing that the "painter of space" survives the death of space itself, and thus to intimate that if Klein were to

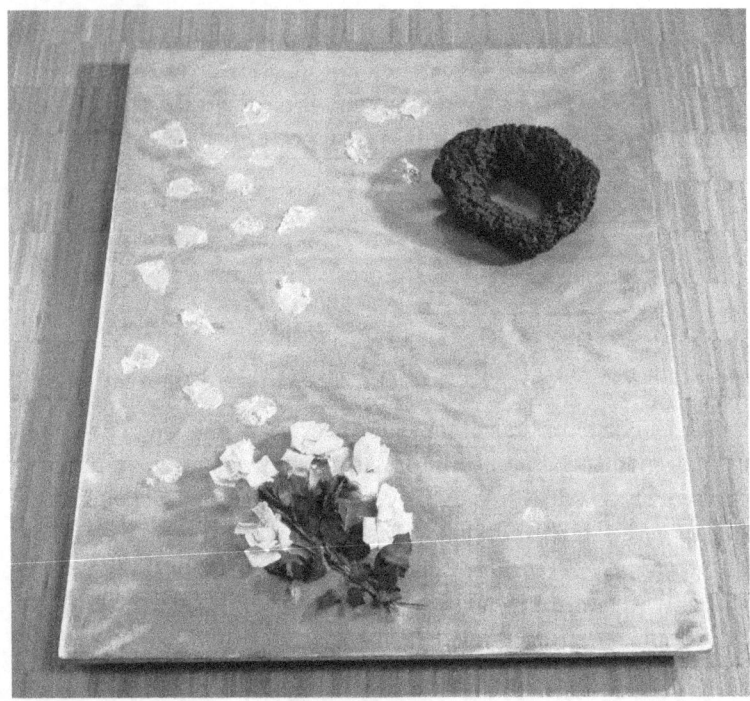

Yves Klein, *Ci-gît l'Espace,* 1960. Photo: CNAC/MNAM/Dist. Réunion des Musées Nationaux / Art Resource, NY © ARS, NY

disappear, immaterial space too would vanish forever. The generosity with which he bequeaths it to his friends, in his real will, reveals his own claim to ownership. He surely knew, since he himself said so, that the fully material oeuvre he would leave behind would be scarcely more than "the ashes of his art."

Today it is hard to see much more in it, unless (like Donald Judd in the 1960s) one ignores whole stretches of his work and forces upon it a formalist reading wholly at variance with its author's intentions, one that doesn't hold up over time. It is, however, equally difficult to make of Klein a detached and sarcastic ironist stripped of illusions, as was Piero Manzoni, whose work answers Klein's point for point and yet, thirty years later, retains all of its acid freshness. It is, finally, even more difficult to set aside the quack in favor of the mystic without sharing beliefs that, once desublimated, fall back upon psychological explanations that are embarrassing in their obviousness.

Not that Joseph Beuys and Andy Warhol were beyond psychology. But their psychology is explained by their works at least as much as it explains them; Klein's work is a symptom. Despite sometimes unequal results, Beuys and Warhol were artists grasping the two ends of a historical contradiction that ran through their work. Even their failure is meaningful and in proportion to their refusal to compromise. Despite and perhaps because of the upsetting nature of his double-headed character—both king and fool—Beuys was an incarnation of history, coming straight out of Shakespeare or Ghelderode. Klein is a creature of history, like the characters in Molière. Despite and perhaps because of his persona's perverse mixture of sadism and compassion, Warhol was a humanist in spite of himself, if we grant that humanism sets in when God withdraws from the world, and glows like an afterimage when money is the only God. Klein was a masochist who believed to have been cleansed of sin because he worshiped a golden calf conceived as *immaterial*. He lacked Beuys's rectitude, his generosity, and the absolute sincerity of his faith in humankind. He was a misanthrope who didn't even have faith in himself. And he lacked Warhol's cold intelligence. He wanted success at least as much as Warhol did, but he had neither his flair for the times nor the instinctual narcissism of one who knows that to make himself desired he must appear entirely without desire. He begged for recognition. He couldn't choose between the star's glamour and the hero's glory, and his pride didn't lead him beyond the triumph of a ham actor on opening night. His ambition was merely social. He couldn't understand that hubris is in the *dépense* and can't be capitalized. He wrestled with the demon of "the hypertrophy of the ego," but the demon threw him. He wanted sainthood, but in the way of the falsely devout who purchase their paradise on earth and indulgences in the beyond.

Indulgence will be granted him only if we first translate his religiosity through his psychic economy (something claimed, alas, by all that art today that invokes mystical experience as its true meaning) and then his psychic economy through the political economy. Here, too, what matters is the congruence of the aesthetic field with the political-economic field—a dated phenomenon for which Klein can do nothing, but which can do something for him. It alone will reanimate the "ashes of his art" and give them their painful and retrospective meaning. The work that sums up Klein is the one thing he hadn't wanted to be a work, his *Ex-Voto* made as an offering to Saint Rita of Cascia. It's a little reliquary in plexiglas divided into five compartments. The three upper ones form a triptych and, from left to right, contain some powdered pink pigment; some *IKB* blue pigment; some gold leaf. The reliquary's lower part is an oblong box containing three little bars of gold resulting from the sale of *Zones of Immaterial Pictorial Sensibility*, set on an *IKB* background. The central part, of the same shape and size, holds an accordion-pleated manuscript dedicated to St. Rita. The *Ex-Voto* dates from February 1961 and was anonymously deposited by Klein in the Monastery of St. Rita of Cascia, in Umbria, immediately after the opening of his Krefeld retrospective. The text, whose first paragraph alone is legible within the casket, was unfurled several years ago by Pierre Restany, Klein's appointed censer-bearer. One can thus overcome one's hesitance to quote a prayer that the artist certainly intended to remain secret. It says a great deal more than a lot of his public declarations had stated. Here is a first excerpt, its undoubtedly sincere humility failing to disguise its naive arrogance:

> Saint Rita of Cascia, I ask thee to intercede with God the Almighty Father that he may always grant me in the name of the Son Jesus Christ and in the name of the Holy Spirit and of the Blessed Virgin Mary that I may live in my works and that they may become ever more beautiful; and may he grant also that I may discover always continually and regularly new things in art more beautiful every time even though alas I am not always worthy to be a tool to build and create Great Beauty. That everything that comes out of me be Beautiful. Amen. Y. K.[1]

A second excerpt, almost touching in its childishness, goes: "That my enemies may become my friends, and if that is impossible that

---

1. Yves Klein, "Prayer to Saint Rita," trans. W. G. Ryan, in *Yves Klein* (Houston: Houston Institute for the Arts, Rice University / New York: Arts Publisher, 1982), 257.

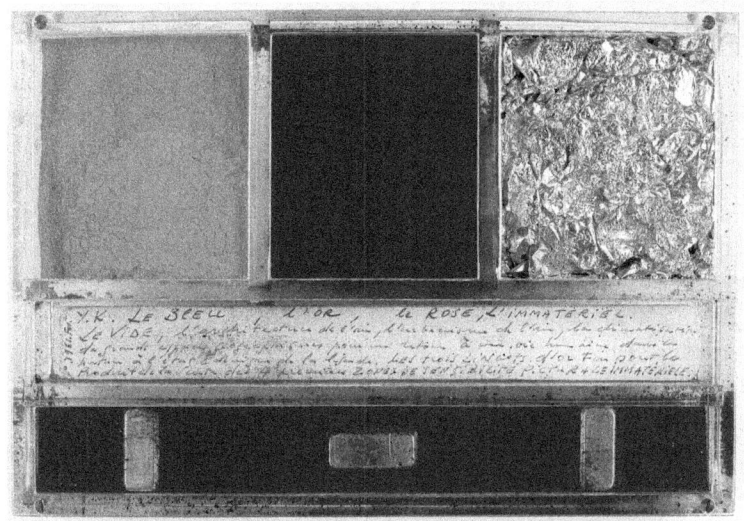

Klein, Ex-voto dédié à sainte Rita de Cascia (recto), 1961. Photograph courtesy of Yves Klein Archives, Paris. © ARS, NY

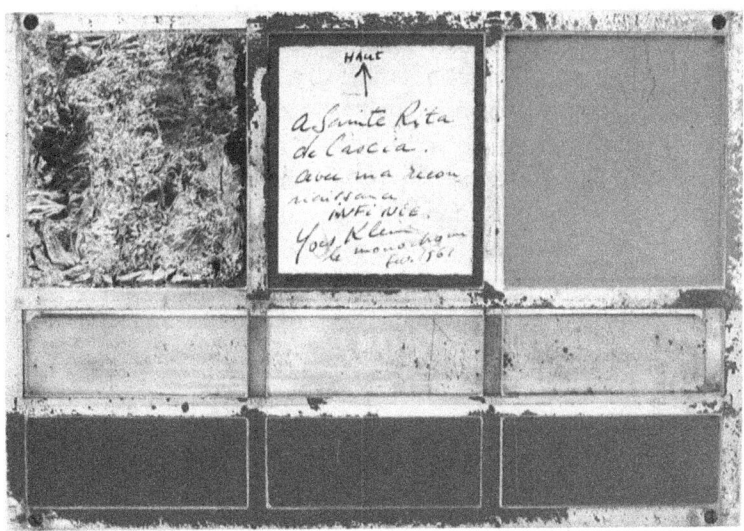

Yves Klein, Ex-voto dédié à sainte Rita de Cascia (verso), 1961. Photograph courtesy of Yves Klein Archives, Paris. © ARS, NY

all they may attempt against me may never result in anything that touches me, ever make me, me and all my works, totally invulnerable. Amen."[2] And a third, of a more than embarrassing megalomania: "That my exhibition at Krefeld may be the greatest success of the century and be recognized by all."[3]

The three excerpts resemble Freud's kettle argument all too well ([1] The kettle is intact; [2] The kettle was damaged already when I borrowed it; [3] I never borrowed your kettle to begin with), as if in order to be the first, one could gamble on the Evangelist's word (the last shall be first), as if true fidelity to oneself did not demand a readiness to endure all reproach, as if it were an act of piety in Job to sit calculating on his dung heap. Grace, if we believe in it, can be received but never requested. Between Klein the mystic and Klein the mystifier there is no choice. He is both of these at once, the first because of the second and the second because of the first, but he incarnates neither. If he is a mystic it's because his greatest talent lies in self-mystification to the point of credulity. And if he is a mystifier, it's because he is wholly sincere in making others believe that he is a mystic, and even more so in making them doubt his sincerity. His life and work abound in ex-votos because everything in them is on the order of vows and wishes, and because the kettle argument is, with a tedious regularity that bespeaks a certain genius, the mainspring of his artistic wishful thinking. When in 1954 Klein published a little monograph titled *Yves Peintures*, supposedly his first "retrospective," the question whether he really painted and exhibited in his hotel rooms in London and Tokyo the monochromes he now reproduced by means of cut papers—whose sizes (reading in millimeters rather than centimeters) referred to themselves rather than to the putative pictures—is a red herring. If he really made them, he demonstrates his precocity and the authenticity of his mystique of the monochrome. If he didn't do them, he shows the clear irony with which he makes fun of *art informel*. If we accuse him of fraudulence, the work retorts that all the hallmarks of fraud were there to be read; and their presence is proof that the artist doesn't cheat. The episode of the cyclist, sometimes present, sometimes absent,

2. Ibid.
3. Ibid.

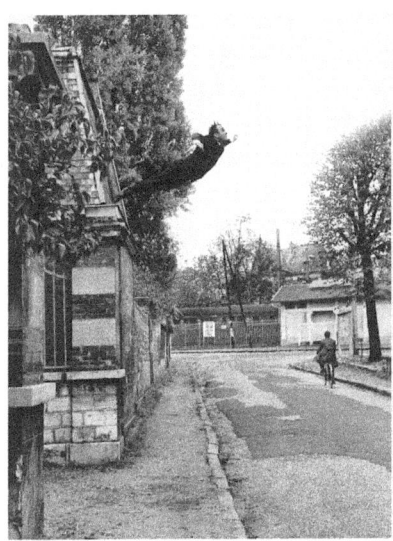 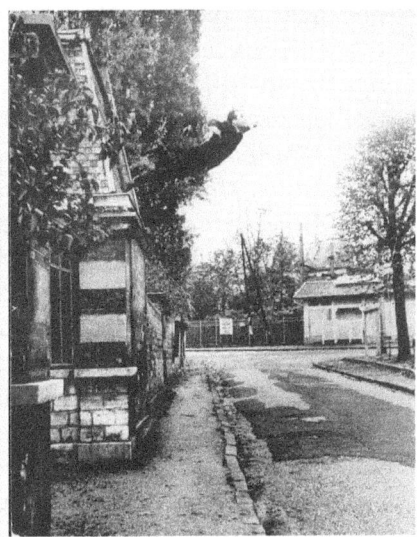

Yves Klein, *Le Saut dans le vide*, 1960. Action artistique d'Yves Klein. Photo Harry Shunk-John Kender. © Yves Klein, ADAGP, Paris. Photograph Shunk-Kender © Roy Lichtenstein Foundation

from the various publications of the *Painter of Space Jumping into the Void* photograph is cut from the same cloth. Either Klein is flying and is gifted with supernatural power, and we must believe the photo; or he jumps and breaks his nose, and we must admire his courage or his talent at landing, like the good judoka he is. Did he trick the photograph? What's the big deal? Either he has constructed an image like any other artist, and the art is in the symbolic power and the magic of his fiction; or he wanted us to notice the fakery, and the art is in the doubt and the reflection sustained by it.

It's the circularity of the kettle argument with Klein, the logic of his "tails I win, heads you lose," which in the final analysis renders him pathetic and distinguishes him from his alter ego, Manzoni. If you remark that his ultramarine, despite its undeniable seductiveness and a real, irradiant power, becomes simply an *effect* through repetition, he says that you haven't really seen it and that all his paintings are different. If, in the grip of this advice, you pay sustained attention to their differences of facture and size, he jeers and pretends that they are all the same. If you insist and ask him why, if this is the case, he's made so many of them, he wiggles out by saying that pictorial quality is immaterial and invisible, and that between two identical monochromes one can be impregnated with it, the other not. And if you don't want to submit to the artist's fiat, you are not sensitive enough to see the invisible.

Is Klein aware of the slips of the tongue in his circular logic? Here are two, which lead—beyond psychology—to economics. Telling about *L'epoca blù*, the Milan exhibition of 1957, in a text that runs the circle described above several times, he gives out this declaration with the artful candor that is his trademark: "Of course the prices were all different." And a little further: "Thus I am looking for the real value of the picture." He is the first to be stunned that the buyers will pay different prices for identical pictures and concludes: "it demonstrates that the pictorial quality of each painting was perceivable by means of something else besides the material appearance . . . ; those who chose recognized this state of things which I call pictorial sensibility." The buyers paid out unequal sums without batting an eye because they are gifted with a very special feeling for the "real value" and recognize that the prices were fair. *Value* and *price* are conflated in a perfect congruence.

After Beuys, after Warhol, the Klein case shows a third type of congruence between the aesthetic field and that of political economy. With Beuys, the congruence is forged by the identification of the artist with the proletarian and the assimilation of labor power to creativity. With Warhol, it is forged through the artist's identification with the machine and the assimilation of the work of art to a commodity, but one without value. With Klein, it is forged by the assimilation of artistic value to value plain and simple, that is, to exchange value, and thus by means of the artist's identification with the capitalist, the dealer, the owner of the means of production. In this equation of values, price is the middle term. For in the aesthetic myth that Klein constructs, the work's price is not what it objectively is, to wit, the measure of scarcity and monopoly. (If it had been, Klein would not have succeeded in selling identical monochromes at different prices, and even less the void.) The price is only the expression of exchange value. No one has succeeded like Klein in isolating, under the name of pictorial quality (on the side of supply) or pictorial sensibility (on the side of demand), the pure exchange value of a work of art as commodity. That's why he was right to regard the true value of his art as immaterial ("exchange value as such doesn't contain matter in a natural state," Marx says) and right, as well, to consider that his works, in their materiality, are "the ashes of his art."

But it's also why he did a considerable wrong to the avant-gardes (a retroactive wrong, one name of which is "neo-avant-garde"). You can't want to be Malevich and Duchamp both at once while all the time vehemently denying the influence of either. Nothing shows this better than when we place the work of Klein—whose parents were both painters—in its own genealogy, when we compare it to its historical antecedents, and when we try to appreciate him formally, as we have to do. He had his *International Klein Blue* patented, and he claimed paternity for monochrome painting, but not without showing, through the virulence of his denials, that he was aware of Rodchenko and Strzeminski. He claimed property rights over the sky's blue, over pictorial space, over the immaterial void, but not without betraying, in his pretension of willing them away, that he had himself received them as a heritage. He hired models whom he used as "living paintbrushes" and actors whom he asked to go about their daily lives considered as a theater performance signed Yves Klein. He systematically acted as the owner of the means of artistic production, as if such a thing were possible. In reality, it was the only path remaining open to him once he had conflated pictorial quality with exchange value. The wrong he committed against the avant-gardes was committed, above all, against himself.

In the passage of the *Critique of Political Economy* where the future theory of commodity fetishism is sketched, Marx is ironic about the way modern economists believe they have escaped the mystification (his word) of the commodity and "sneer at the illusions of the Monetary System," even while when they "deal with the more complex economic categories, such as capital, they display the same illusions. This emerges clearly in the confession of naive astonishment when the phenomenon that they have just ponderously described as a thing reappears as a social relation and, a moment later, having been defined as a social relation, teases them once more as a thing."[4]

4. Karl Marx, *A Contribution to the Critique of Political Economy*, trans. S. W. Ryazanskaya (New York: International Publishers, 1970), 35.

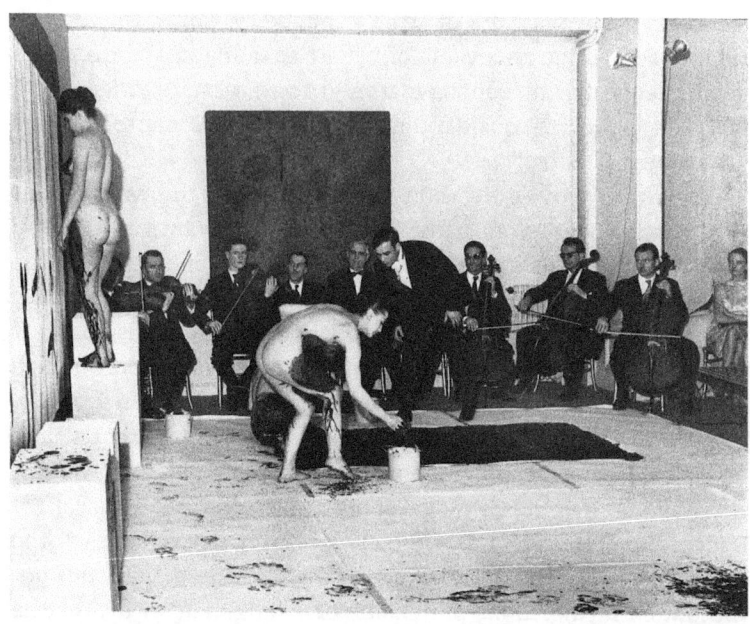

Yves Klein, *Anthropométries de l'époque bleue*, Galerie Internationale d'art contemporain, Paris, 9 March 1960. © Yves Klein, ADAGP, Paris; Photograph Shunk-Kender © Roy Lichtenstein Foundation. Photograph courtesy of Yves Klein Archives, Paris

Mystified mystifier, Klein is, like these economists, the theologian of the artistic commodity, despite himself. The "real value of the picture" is invisible; it could only be the hidden social relation that is later to be brutally revealed through its price. The price, in turn, is the expression of the exchange value that the transaction itself presents as a social relation, only to be hidden again in the materiality of the picture. At the very moment when the buyer believes that he is acquiring immaterial pictorial value, it is a vulgar monetary quantity that soon returns to sneer at him, substituting for a banal painted object in which the seller no longer recognizes anything but the ashes of his art. Like the bourgeois economists, Klein sees only the purely exchangelike nature of this social relation because he conflates value with price. Now price does not incorporate labor, whereas value does. And it's almost by a slip of the tongue that the truth comes out, while his work is pervaded with the "metaphysical

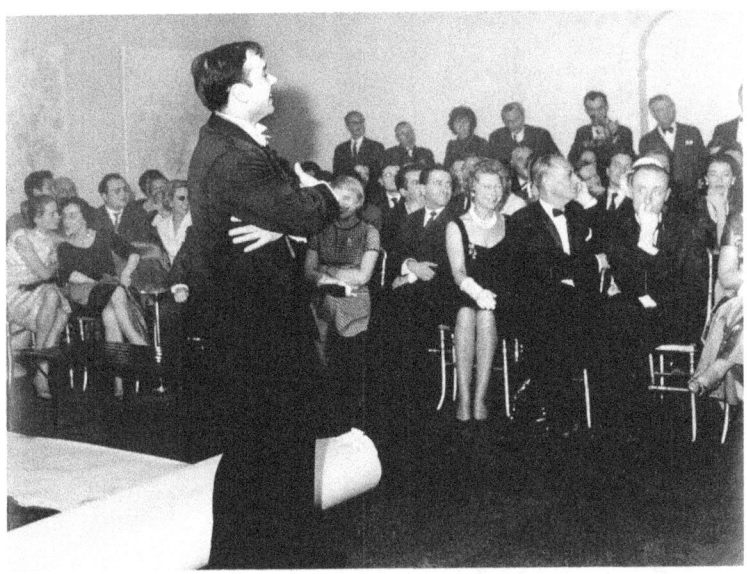

Yves Klein, *Anthropométries de l'époque bleue*, Galerie Internationale d'art con-
temporain, Paris, 9 March 1960. © Yves Klein, ADAGP, Paris; Photograph Shunk-
Kender © Roy Lichtenstein Foundation. Photograph courtesy of Yves Klein Archives,
Paris

and theological capers" of the fetish. The value in question, he says,
resides in the incommensurable difference between two identical
objects, "one of them, however, painted by a painter and the other
by a skilled technician, an artisan." The price difference is supposed
to measure the incommensurable and to prove that "one of the two
objects is a picture, the other not." There's where the trap of wishful
thinking closes over Yves-the-monochrome. While Beuys instantiates art in will and Warhol in desire, Klein instantiates it in avowal
or pretension, on the self-proclamation of the artist. He whose only
tangible contribution to the history of painting is the chemical formula that allowed him to fix powdered pigment without diminish-
ing its glow, asks us to take him at his word when he pronounces
himself a painter instead of judging him on his works, even when
the pictures are beautiful. He who was above all a skilled technician

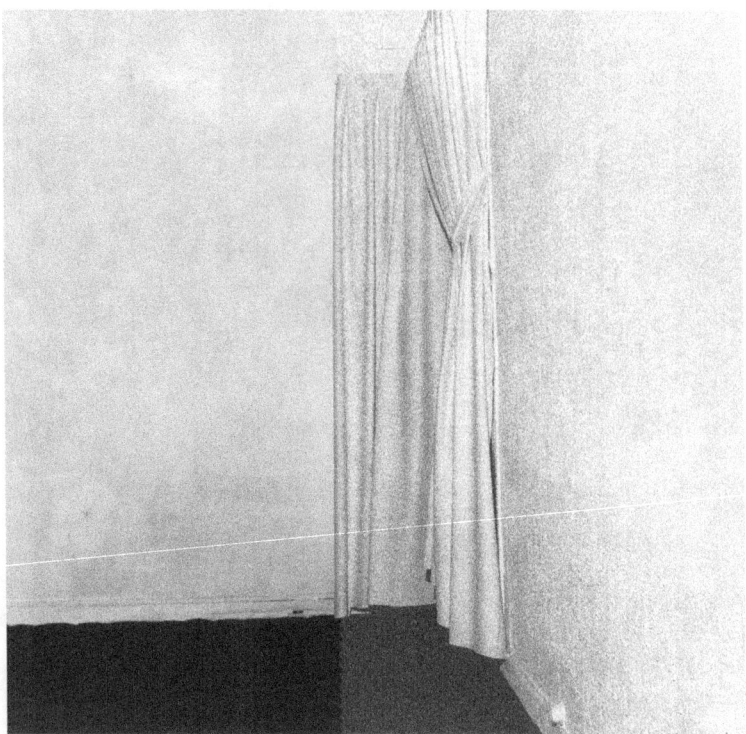

Yves Klein, *La Spécialisation de la sensibilité picturale à l'état matière première en sensibilité picturale stabilisée (Le Vide)*. Galerie Iris Clert, Paris, 28 April–12 May 1958. Photo: Unknown Photograph courtesy of Yves Klein Archives, Paris © ARS, NY

and a tireless artisan proclaims himself a painter through the force of wishful thinking. How do we know if he is one? The artisan works, the painter doesn't: "I will be a painter. They will say about me: there's the painter. And I will feel myself to be a painter, a true one precisely because I won't paint, or at least to all appearances. The fact that I exist as a painter will be the most powerful pictorial work of this age."

Beuys worked and wanted, in working, to actualize a creative potential present in every human being, not to produce exchange value. That his work had a price would have to disappear with the coming of his economic system. His artistic fame, far from being a privileged status, was meant to point the way of liberation for all to become fully what they already were. Warhol, too, worked but, in wanting to act like a machine, revealed the fact that in reality no artist works (i.e., produces exchange value), and that the status of all artists is to exist as prized but valueless commodities, that their fame, far from being a proof of personal talent or the emergence of a universal creativity, is the price that their signatures will fetch when their work, over which their dealer has a monopoly, is in demand. Klein, too, worked but wanted it to be his existence and not his activity to which both value and price would be attached; he wanted his status as artist to justify his fame and prove his talent, to have the monopoly over creativity, and the buyer (not the viewer) to have the monopoly over aesthetic pleasure. When he claims not to work, it is not, like Warhol, in order to signify that no painter produces exchange value; quite to the contrary, it is to assert that he is the only one able to produce exchange value without working. And when he claims that his existence as a painter "will be the most powerful pictorial work of this age," it is not, like Beuys, in order to signify that all human existence, because it is creative in essence, can actualize itself in an artwork; to the contrary, it is in order to appropriate human essence, that is, creativity or labor power, by not actualizing it. He, too, interprets Beuys's equation "creativity = capital," but it's capital as accumulation and creativity as private property.

We can see the retroactive wrong Klein commits against the avant-gardes who believed in the liberating power of creativity and wanted to give art its use value: he claims to appropriate the universal for himself and to sell it by the piece; and the only thing he calls art is exchange value. We also see what wrong he committed against himself: universality is not divisible and is not for sale. To believe that one could possess it is worse than wishful thinking, it is a sin against humankind; and to believe that exchange value is sui generis is the error of a theologian-economist. Klein, the painter who doesn't work, is forced to exploit Klein, the working artisan, to alienate his labor power and to reify his production. He deserves to have his Tartuffe-like piety turned round against him, to have all his work reduced to an ex-voto; he deserves to be taken at his word with a refusal to judge the "ashes of his art" aesthetically, even when they are beautiful, which they often are.Whence then might he receive indulgence? Perhaps from the fact that the wrong he committed against both himself and the avant-gardes is one that he has suffered at the hands of these same avant-gardes: from the very fact that they were demanding reparations for a wrong that can't be proved. Klein's mystical *Schwärmereien* are perhaps not his alone, and he was perhaps more lucid about the avant-garde's liberating utopias than we might think. Creativity is, after all, only a myth, and Klein lets this be understood by systematically repeating himself, by denying originality, by inviting accusations of fraudulence. The alliance of art and utility in order to achieve a happy society was, after all, nothing but another myth, and in saluting "the functionalists, martyrs of the most beautiful of myths: the equation of happiness," Klein showed he was not the dupe of this alliance.

Now creativity is *labor power* and utility is *use value*. It is in Marx's text that we find articulated, with the strongest rational conviction, the concepts that resonate throughout all of artistic modernity—this mythical fabric woven in a hundred ways by a warp thread pulled from economics and a woof thread from aesthetics. To it we must therefore return one more time, crossing the writings of his youth with those of his maturity and recalling that in the latter the two key concepts of labor power and use value are introduced precisely to surreptitiously restore the meaning of the abandoned concept of alienation. They serve as well to justify politically that the wrongs committed against producers and consumers through alienation and reification must still be redressed. Labor power and use value represent the debt of the "scientific" Marx to the "romantic" and Hegelian Marx. It is thus Marx's conception of labor that most clearly reveals the wrong his anthropology—which defined man as *homo faber* and social ties as relations of production—committed against the utopias of those many righters of wrongs who would perhaps not even have recognized him as one of their own.

What, then, is labor for Marx? On the one hand, it is the actualization of labor power, the implementation of the productive force that defines human essence, the qualitative movement through which humankind appropriates or reappropriates its essence. On the other hand, it is the substance of all exchange value, the quantitative *Dasein* of human productivity when it is measured by time, which quantifies the *wertbildende Substanz* (value-building substance) incorporated in a commodity. In both cases, labor is general or generic. But not for the same reasons. Labor power is universal, existing "before" division of labor and traversing all social forms. Its actualization identifies generically with the advent of the individual human being as *Gattungswesen*. We find ourselves, so to speak, on that side of the divide where nothing is yet commodity, where, de jure if not de facto, usage is master, and where, even alienated, the implementation of labor power is potentially disalienated, for it is exactly this potential for disalienation that labor actualizes. With labor as substance creating exchange value, we are, on the contrary, on the other side of the divide. Here everything is already commodity; use is deferred; time equalizes what it measures because it is subsequent to the division of labor, making concrete labor an abstraction. Monetary exchange, not human nature, is the one and only universal.

To these general or generic forms correspond specialized or specific forms. On the one hand, without ceasing to actualize labor force in general, labor as the creator of use value is always the exercise of a specialized trade or a specific skill, producing a given product for a given use. This labor is concrete, Marx says, and immanent to social relations of production that are themselves concrete, to a division of labor that Marx goes so far as to call natural, resulting from the needs of the community and the customs and skills of its members. It is this labor and these specific relations of production that Marx projects hypothetically onto primitive communism and utopically onto the communism of the future. On the other hand, while still remaining the labor that Marx calls undifferentiated, common, simple, homogeneous, general, and abstract, labor as creator of exchange value takes on these characterizations only in contrast with what it ought to be, what it would be if it weren't alienated, and what it potentially is anyway, as creator of use value, albeit deferred by and for exchange. Alienation is the specific mode of existence of labor, and reification constitutes the specific relations of production, in the conditions—themselves specific—of capitalism and the market economy. In vain did the "scientific," mature Marx abandon the concept of alienation (or via Steuart give it a non-Hegelian content). What remained constant is that he kept attributing to the dialectical contradiction between the generality and the specificity of labor the task of justifying the theoretical possibility of surpassing capitalism and the practical necessity of so doing. How indeed can we justify class struggle, armed revolution, or the dictatorship of the proletariat if the still-to-be-invented specificity of the future communist society doesn't promise to hold equally for all, to emancipate not a particular social class but humankind as a whole? And how are we to prove that the universality of the commodity and of capitalist exchange is surpassable without first demonstrating that it is only relative to a particular historical situation and the domination of a specific social class? It falls to labor power—postulated as generic, that is, as transcendent to individuals and social classes—to justify in practice the specificity of the emancipated society. And it falls to use value—postulated as specific, that is, immanent to the customs and the needs of individuals within society—to justify in theory the possibility of general or generic emancipation.

Labor power and use value are postulates, ideas, transcendentals, and as such undemonstrable. That each person is gifted with creativity, that labor emancipate him or her, and that emancipation in return free labor is a practical, or "praxical," or political postulate. It's a generous postulate, but nonetheless a postulate. That labor has the satisfaction of a need as its purpose, and that in return a quest for utility guides labor, is a theoretical, or scientific, or ideological postulate. It's a rational postulate, but nonetheless a postulate. They could have remained independent of each other. It was not necessary that the actualization of labor power aim for utility; Bataille, for example, focused it on expenditure. It was not necessary that needs (or desires) find the prime cause of satisfaction in labor; Freud, for example, looked for it in sexuality. But with Marx, the dialectic of the specific and the general insists that one of the two postulates entails the other, and this mutual entailment means in return that the theoretical flows dialectically into the practical and the practical into the theoretical. It is there that the postulates, undemonstrable as they should remain, make a claim to be demonstrable and harden into dogma and doctrines. *Dialectic* is the name of the wrong directly or indirectly caused by Marx, by Marxism or the Marxisms, and by other parallel emancipatory utopias. We have seen too many historically confirmed examples, including the caricature summed up by the maxim "Without a correct theory no just practice, without just practice no correct theory." Who cannot but see a particularly tragic form there—and on what a scale!—of circular wishful thinking?

Psychology doesn't explain everything. Klein surely had, psychologically, just what it took to be this illusionist who deluded himself through wishful thinking. But like Beuys and Warhol, he too testified. His personal wishful thinking emerges at a precise moment in history (one of those moments that Marx—him again—had characterized as the return of tragedy in the guise of farce), in this case, the repetition of the "historical" avant-gardes in the parodic disguise of the postwar neo-avant-gardes. (Beuys's effort seems all the more heroic in comparison, but just as vain, in having tried to give farce the dignity of tragedy again.) It is this historical moment that gives a single, exclusively economic hue to the palette of Yves-the-monochrome and forces him to recycle unconsciously and in parody a wishful thinking that was not his alone but also that of the "historical" avant-gardes, and of many a brand of Marxism as well. Klein, ironically, testified to the failure of the avant-gardist utopias; he unwittingly volunteered to shoulder the wrong that they had in fact done to themselves with the presumption that only identification with the proletarian was just and liberating. It's not that he was lacking in utopias—the blue revolution, universal levitation—but they were already mere parodies of utopia. His pathos borders on the tragic insofar as the debacle of utopia left him no choice but to embody parodically all the wrongdoers and thus to see, ironically, all the wrongs turn round against him. In identifying himself with the owners of the means of production, he assumed the sins of the capitalist. He embodied that which causes the alienation of the proletarian and the reification of commodities, capital, and even capital in its "ultimate" stage, monopoly state capitalism. It was unjust—no one has the right of ownership over the artistic means of production—but true. It is, however, true only insofar as ownership of the artistic means of production is possible; otherwise it's merely ridiculous. In other words: if it is true that humankind is defined in its essence by creativity and that it is robbed by the regime of private property; if it is true that we resist exchange value only by holding fast to use value; if it is true that alienation and reification are wrongs; if it is true that Beuys and the artistic lineage he embodies are right. Or again, if the Marxist utopia is just and Marxist theory correct; if it is both just and true that a circular dialectic between the specific and the generic "proves" practice by means of theory and vice versa.

For modern art, one of the names of the specific is *painting*, and the name of the generic is *art*. Their circular dialectic turns to parody in the work and behavior of Yves Klein, whose dilemma lay in his unwillingness to choose between "being a painter" and "playing the artist," and whose wishful-thinking solution was to prove that he was the one because he played the other, and vice versa. To be a *painter* he had to paint, to practice a specific trade as an artisan. But Klein wanted the price of his pictures to measure their exchange value exclusively, and exchange value is general. Thus he posed as an *artist* and exhibited the void—what could be more general? He played the card of art's social ritual in the context of a commercial gallery where ordinarily what gets exchanged is painting for money, specific aesthetic value for a general equivalent. He still had to establish that this exchange actually bartered the specific against the general. He titled the exhibition *The Specialization of Sensibility in the State of Raw Material into Stabilized Pictorial Sensibility*. He thus worked, like a specialized artisan (indeed he repainted the gallery white). Yet he still had to cash in the general in order to prove that an exchange had occurred. Therefore he forced the visitors who didn't have an invitation card to pay: "Although all the pictorial sensibility is for sale in shards or in a single block, through impregnation, visitors, consciously or not, will be able to rob me of a certain degree of intensity, despite myself. And that, that above all, that must be paid for." If aesthetic value is exchange value, only the buyers have the right to it. In return, only the purchase proves that *stabilized pictorial sensibility* has value and that Klein is a painter. He probably thought, however, after the exhibition of *The Void* at Iris Clert's gallery in 1958 that the process was inelegant and, what's more, incoherent: why shouldn't visitors with invitation cards also have to recognize their debt to this artist who calls himself a painter because he possesses pictorial sensibility and doesn't use it to make pictures? With the *Ritual Rules for the Transfer of Zones of Immaterial Pictorial Sensibility*, he would refine the demonstration. This time pictorial sensibility is called *immaterial* rather than *specialized*

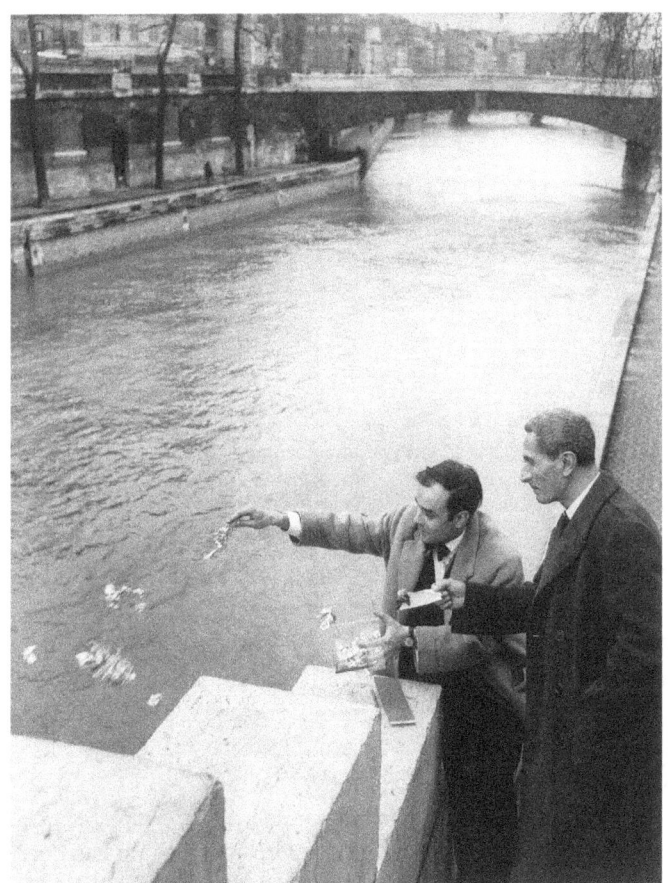

Yves Klein, Cession à Dino Buzzati de la "Zone de sensibilité picturale immatérielle" n°5, série n°1, Paris, Pont-au-Double, 26 January 1962. © Yves Klein, ADAGP, Paris. Photograph Shunk-Kender © Roy Lichtenstein Foundation

from a *state of raw material*. Klein no longer paints (not even the gallery white), he is a painter. He no longer sells anything specific but transfers pure general exchange value. How will we know that it is *pictorial*? Specificity shifts onto the side of money: no more payment in currency, but in gold. How will we know that exchange has really taken place? Klein delivers a receipt to the buyer. But the receipt is nothing but "ashes": "every future buyer of a zone of immaterial pictorial sensibility should know that the simple fact of

CACHET DE GARANTIE

SÉRIE N° 1   N°   03

*Reçu Vingt Grammes d'Or Fin
contre une Zone de Sensibilité Picturale Immatérielle*

CETTE ZONE TRANSFÉRABLE NE PEUT ÊTRE CÉDÉE PAR
SON PROPRIÉTAIRE QU'AU DOUBLE DE SA VALEUR
D'ACHAT INITIALE.
(SIGNATURES ET DATES POUR TRANSFERTS AU DOS).
LE TRANSGRESSEUR S'EXPOSE A L'ANNIHILATION TOTALE
DE SA PROPRE SENSIBILITÉ.

Yves Klein, reçu donné à Paride Accetti pour l'achat de la "Zone de sensibilité picturale immatérielle" n°3, série n°1 (7 December 1959). Photograph courtesy of Yves Klein Archives, Paris © ARS, NY

accepting a receipt for the price he has paid deprives him of all authentic immaterial value of the work, even though he is the possessor of it." The receipt must then be reduced to ashes for the allegiance of the buyer to the fiat of the artist to be complete. Then the artist throws half the gold into the sea or the river. "From this moment on, the zone of immaterial pictorial sensibility belongs in an absolute and intrinsic manner to the buyer."

"Klein Sells Wind!" runs the headline of a newspaper. A fool's bargain? Not really. Neither side is wronged. Nothing has been reified, no one is alienated. Klein has pocketed half the gold, but after all it's the painter-artist in him who exploits the artist-painter. Without the "ashes," the "art" would not have found a buyer. The latter has nothing? He has received grace, and that's a lot to a believer. There remains for him to associate his prayer to that of Yves Klein and to slide it, like the gold of the sale, into the *Ex-Voto* that the artist is ready to deposit at the feet of St. Rita. But who is St. Rita? The *transfer* is null and void if it didn't take place "in the presence of a museum director, or a known art dealer, or an art critic, plus two witnesses." Behold St. Rita. When the mapping of the aesthetic field onto that of political economy attains perfect congruence, St. Rita takes the form of the representatives of art-as-commerce. These are the owners of the means of production, the possessors of the monopoly of the sensibility for artistic exchange value. The dealer in wind is dead, and he didn't want his material work to survive him, preferring that his estate be handled by other merchants of the immaterial as devout as he. But when the mapping of the aesthetic and the economic is so perfectly congruent, its historical dialectic is over, and dialectic itself turns to parody. The judgment by which something is called art (or good art, or significant art) has no more—and no less—to do with values than it had to do with piety and devotion in the days when the field of aesthetics was congruent with the field of religion. Klein shows this despite himself, and it's the only indulgence his ex-votos will have gained him.

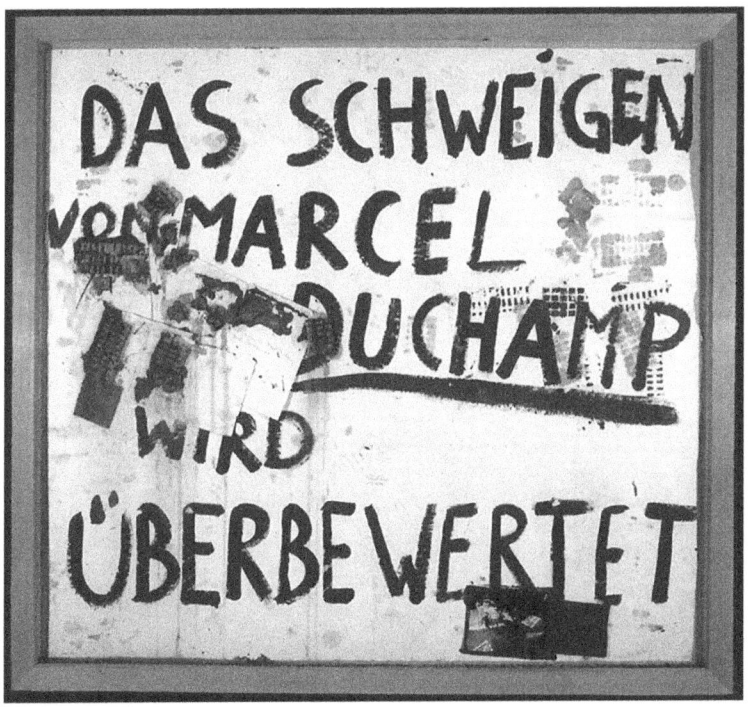

Joseph Beuys, *Das Schweigen von Marcel Duchamp wird überbewertet,* board from the action *The Silence of Marcel Duchamp Is Overrated,* 1964. © 2012 Artists Rights Society (ARS), New York / VG Bild-Kunst, Bonn

Marcel Duchamp, or The Phynancier of Modern Life

In the whole of the twentieth century, there is no less utopian an artist than Marcel Duchamp. And there is no artist—with the exception of Matisse, whom Duchamp greatly admired—who suffered less from the failing of utopias. Never did Duchamp believe that art had it in its power to promise a better, more just, or happier society, and never did he have to regret that art had reneged on its promises. Long before Yves Klein began selling wind, Duchamp cruelly projected the idea of "establish[ing] a society in which the individual has to pay for the air he breathes," while quietly, tongue in cheek, continuing to lead the life of a *respirateur* (breather). Long before Andy Warhol went shopping and stacked up fake boxes of Brillo, he bought a real bottle rack from a department store and simply waited for time to make it into art and for viewers to give it a price. Long before Joseph Beuys declared that "the silence of Marcel Duchamp is overrated," he stopped talking and let others estimate the worth of his silence. He had understood that all the utopias of modernity had already been realized and thus that they had never been utopias.

Beuys was right; it is true that everyone is a potential artist. But does that guarantee that creativity and use value even exist? No one knows; these are but ideas, postulates. Nothing says that everyone is endowed with a productive faculty that is presently alienated but that defines or will define humanity in its generic essence. And nothing proves that it is just, as a matter of principle, that everyone be an artist, or liberating that everyone will someday become one. Nothing says that humans must work in order to satisfy their needs and must graft their presently reified relations onto this specific horizon. And nothing proves that it is just and liberating that they do so. Alienation and reification are wrongs to be righted only on the grounds of these postulates. Warhol was also right; it is true that art is a business and the work of art a commodity. But does that mean that creativity and use value do not exist and that one must cynically accept art's absorption into exchange value? After all, Warhol had his utopia as well: if all artists are machines and produce no exchange value, then all consumers are potential art lovers. But that doesn't prove that they will consume well, and it doesn't promise that what tradition called art will survive its commodification. It shows only that Yves Klein was wrong and that it was unjust for the artist to claim to own the means of artistic production and to restrict artistic consumption to the buyer. One can cause and suffer wrongs without one's supporting postulates being proved.

Nothing is proved, then, and it is as if Duchamp, skeptic, took off from these observations. It is as if he had, *in advance*, observed Yves Klein struggling with his wishful thinking and had understood that indeed "to be a painter," or rather to have been one, was the preliminary condition to "playing the artist." This is what his own wish fulfillments had taught him. And it is as if he had, *in advance*, watched Warhol's success and understood that the *spleen* of the commodity was the condition for any object whatsoever to be called art, and that the disappearance of aesthetic value into exchange value was the condition for such an object to have a price. It is what the success of his readymades had taught him. It is as if he had watched Beuys play the père Ubu of creativity and had understood that at the moment when the artist-proletarian saw himself brought home to a bohemia as unreal as Jarry's Poland, the congruence of the aesthetic field with that of political economy had been perfect, complete, accomplished. *Etant donné* this lesson, only one question remained: how to make art out of *that*?

The reference to Jarry is anything but accidental, when we know with what grains of irony *Marchand du sel* seasoned the formula through which he "defined" art: "Arrhe est à art ce que merdre est à merde" (Arrhe is to art as shitte is to shit). There's nothing left to say; it is not art but rather the very congruence of art with economy that the formula analyzes by means of "algebraic comparison."

There are hundreds of ways to read that formula, one of which is as follows: *arrhe*,[1] as Duchamp practices it, is to art as practiced by the modernists who believe in utopias what King Ubu's swear word, *merdre* (which is also the first word of *Ubu Roi*), is to the substance whose retention fashions the "anal-sadistic" tendencies of all the capitalist misers of the world. The grain of salt that would allow this substance to be taken for a secretion of an artist's creativity is gross indeed. But when everyone can be an artist simply by free access to the marketplace where what is reified on the one hand gets sublimated on the other, the odds are heavy that a large part of what gets traded there is in the nature of the substance in question. (Manzoni didn't miss the opportunity to remind the all too sublime Yves Klein of this.) And since on this market the artist is a proletarian who alienates his labor power (Beuys's version), or a machine churning out things that, though without value, have a price (Warhol's), why not kill two birds with one stone and make one's body into "a transformer designed to utilize the slight, wasted energies such as . . . the fall of urine and excrement"? Provided the artist knows how to exploit the unexpected—and least prodigal—resources of his labor power, he will always find himself some businessman or other able to turn a profit from the few quanta of *wertbildende Substanz* nevertheless spent. Besides, it's better to take care of that oneself. Laziness is the best of foremen and the most fertile of inventors, and humor the most efficient of dealers. It's up to the worker or the machine to supply the *waterfall*, and up to the dealer to pay the bill for the *illuminating gas*. *Etant donné*, then, these two conditions—labor and commerce, the field of political economy—how to make *arrhe* out of that?

In New York, in April 1917, a so-called R. Mutt submits a urinal titled *Fountain* to the hanging committee (of which Duchamp was chair) of the newly created Society of Independent Artists, Incorporated. The Society, whose motto was "No jury, no prizes," was open on principle to everyone: the membership card cost a dollar, the annual dues, five. For this modest sum, and on the additional condition of showing the year of their joining up, Mr. or Mrs. Nobody

1. Translator's note: *les arrhes* (a plural noun), which means a deposit or down payment, is homophonic with *art* in French.

arrhe est à art ceque
merdre est à merde.

$$\frac{arrhe}{art} = \frac{merdre}{merde}$$

grammaticᵉˡᵉᵐᵗ :
l'arrhe de la peinture est du
~~fém~~ genre feminin

Marcel Duchamp, *Boîte de 1914*—Arrhe est à art, 1914. © 2012 Artists Rights Society (ARS), New York / ADAGP, Paris / Succession Marcel Duchamp

became, in a certain sense, a stockholder of the Société Anonyme (the name would be used by Duchamp in 1920 for the collection he created with Katherine Dreier), from which, on the whole, all American artists exposed to the ostracism of the National Academy hoped to receive dividends. Mr. or Mrs. Nobody is thus simultaneously a small-time capitalist in an enterprise licensed to deal in art (the exhibited works were for sale) and an independent artisan otherwise invited to display his or her know-how. Marcel Duchamp shared this double status with the thousand or so self-proclaimed artists who participated in the 1917 exhibition, except that he played on one side as on the other an ascendant role. On the stockholders' side, he was one of the twenty founding members and, to boot, chair of the hanging committee; on the artisans' side, he was recognized for his talent as a painter, being the author of the highly celebrated *Nude Descending a Staircase*. Yet giving up this double privilege and playing Mr. Nobody, he submitted his entry under a pseudonym. The urinal was refused. Duchamp kept quiet, waited for the storm

to pass, and at the close of the show published in his little satiri-
cal review, *The Blind Man*, an unsigned editorial titled "The Richard
Mutt Case," which, taking up R. Mutt's defense, also reveals his first
name.

Duchamp didn't make the *Fountain* with his own hands, like
an artisan; he bought it from its manufacturer, the J. L. Mott Iron
Works. The name Mutt signals this provenance with little disguise.
"And I added Richard," Duchamp said. "That's not a bad name for a
pissotière. Get it? The opposite of poverty." He couldn't have been
more explicit. The signature acknowledges the double status of
the nobody who proclaims himself an artist in becoming a member
of the society. On the one side there is the manufacturer, Mutt or
Mott, who stands in for the artisan, and on the other Richard, the
capitalist, the stockholder. It is as if the latter had placed an order
with the former, or rather, as if Richard (alias Duchamp, chair of the
hanging committee), too lazy or too busy with lighting the entries of
his co-stockholders with *illuminating gas*, had charged Mutt (alias
Duchamp, author of *Nude Descending a Staircase*) with painting
The Waterfall, and the latter, hardly less sluggish, had gone to supply himself at J. L. Mott's, whose advertisements ran thus: "Among
our articles of lazy hardware we recommend a faucet which stops
dripping when nobody is listening to it." Mott has the item in stock.
Mutt hands over the deposit while promising to pay the rest as soon
as possible, even adding, quite candidly, that he counts on resell-
ing the object at a profit. "Well, that's a peculiar use for a urinal,"
Mott mutters under his breath, "But it's none of my business. Mine
is to sell things that help men do number one, but I sell for the sake
of selling and not for them to relieve themselves." And the deal is
struck. Whereupon Mutt goes away, his *Fountain* under his arm,
and takes it to Richard and his hanging committee. Richard, just as
lazy an administrator as Mutt is a painter, is absent. His assistants
(George Bellows and Rockwell Kent) throw up their arms and ex-
claim: "The *Fountain* may be a very useful object in its place, but
its place is not an art exhibition and it is, by no definition, a work
of art." (That's the text of the press release published by the orga-
nizers the day after the opening.) The follow-up is very muddled,
and the versions of the facts vary. Here's one (certainly false, but
accredited by Duchamp): Another Richard comes along, a friend of

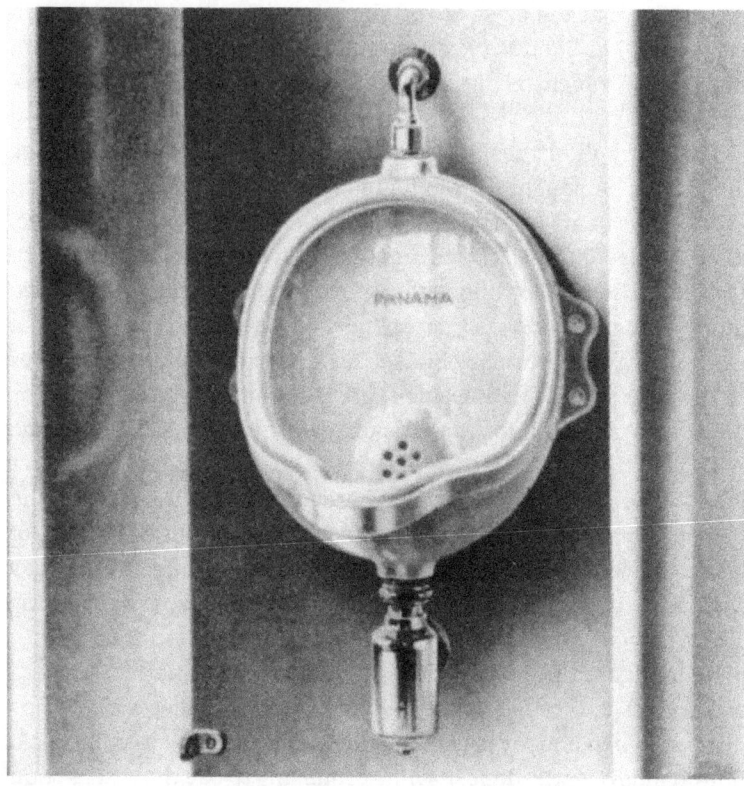

The J. L. Mott Iron Works, "Vitro-Adamant" model urinal, 1907/1908

the first (in fact his name was Walter C. Arensberg, art collector), and asks about the object of the scandal. Nobody seems to know. "I want to buy it, sight unseen!" he bellows. Bellows and Kent find the object behind a partition, and Arensberg, big spender, hands over a blank check, saying, "Fill in the amount yourselves." Upon which, flanked by Duchamp and Man Ray, he leaves the room "holding his new acquisition as though it were a marble Aphrodite." Mutt goes back to Mott's and pays the balance. Richard resigns from the society and never cashes his dividends. Arensberg loses the urinal (if he ever had it). And Duchamp has only to wait. He had his reply to the *speculation* he had jotted down as early as 1913: "Can one make works which are not works of 'art'?" The answer was no, for speculation there had been indeed.

Taking it from the top: *arrhe* is to art what *shitte* is to shit. The art that Mutt practices in working as little as possible but paying *arrhes* to Mott is to the art of those who work and believe in creativity what speculation is to production, what *Phynance* (as Jarry spelled "finance" in *Ubu Roi*) is to political economy. The word *arrhes*, which means deposit or down payment, exists only in the plural. Duchamp writes it in the singular, adding: "Grammatically, the *arrhe* of painting is feminine in gender." Here's how the word becomes triply specific, then: as a name for money, it loses its character of general equivalency and signifies the singular advance on a singular payment; as the homophone for the word *art*, it refers only to painting specifically and not to the arts in general; as a gendered word, it designates only half of humankind and shows it to be female. Now "one only has: for *female* the urinal and one *lives* by it." This is in *The 1914 Box*, three years before *Fountain*. Now, *Virgin* and *Bride* are titles of works between which, in August 1912, Duchamp painted *The Passage from the Virgin to the Bride*, and after which, in October, he gave up painting and found himself a

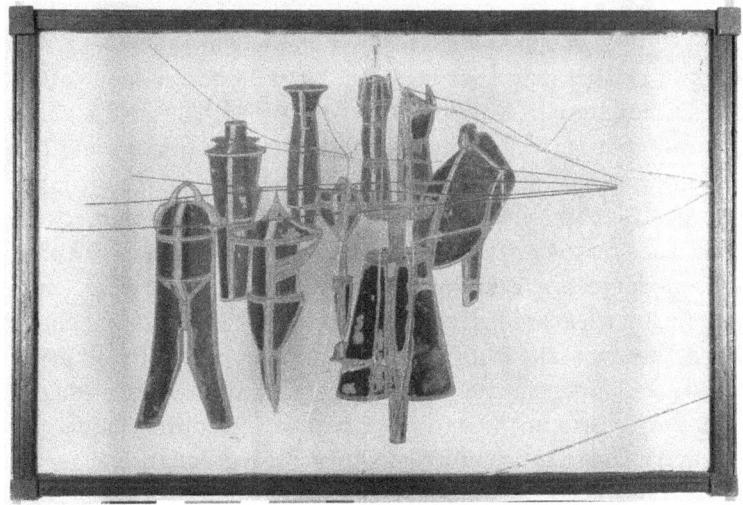

Marcel Duchamp, *Nine Malic Molds* (*Cemetery of Uniforms and Liveries*), 1914-15, private collection. Photo: CNAC/MNAM / Dist. Réunion des Musées Nationaux / Art Resource, NY. © 2012 Artists Rights Society (ARS), New York / ADAGP, Paris / Succession Marcel Duchamp

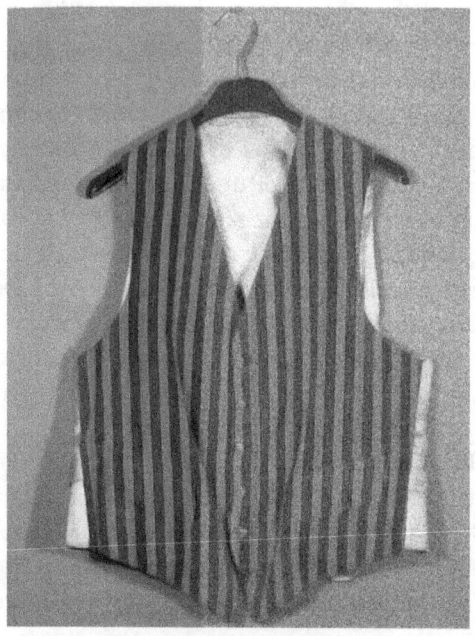

Marcel Duchamp, *Gilet pour Benjamin Péret*, 1958. © 2012 Artists Rights Society (ARS), New York / ADAGP, Paris / Succession Marcel Duchamp

job on the labor market as librarian, "in order to get enough time to paint for myself." Now, of his strange activity as "arrhtist" who paints for himself, who composes random music (*Erratum musical*) and draws plans for his *Large Glass* but doesn't paint any longer, between October 1912 and the 1917 Independents nothing or very little lands on the market where ordinarily the specific work of an artisan-painter is exchanged for general currency. And when *Fountain* (in French *Fontaine*, feminine, just like *Virgin* and *Bride*) makes her appearance, she is no longer the product of either painting or artisanship. Duchamp has made art, period, without its belonging to one of the arts, no more to music or to architecture than to painting, and not even to sculpture. Moreover, he has done nothing at all; he has bought a ready-made object whose manufacturer, J. L. Mott, didn't make either. Those who made the urinal neither made art nor tried to do so; they were the workers whose *creativity* (read: labor power) Mott bought on the labor market.

The word *ready-made* comes from the garment industry. Duchamp didn't invent it; he borrowed it, indeed ready-made, to dress up the snow shovel he had just bought from a New York hardware store in 1915. In the *Theories of Surplus Value* (book 4 of *Capital*), Marx, who liberally supplies himself with examples taken from the industrial avant-garde of his age—and the garment industry is one—differentiates productive from unproductive labor. The artisan-tailor to whom the cloth for a pair of trousers is brought and who is paid for his services is an unproductive worker, he says, while the worker-tailor employed by a merchant-tailor who derives surplus value from his labor is a productive worker. In the same way Mutt, commissioned by Richard to paint a *Waterfall*, is in the situation of Marx's artisan-tailor, and Mott's worker, who fabricates the *Fountain*, is in the situation of his worker-tailor. The artist who works for himself (as Duchamp said), or from inner necessity (as Kandinsky would say), or out of pleasure, or for posterity, is an unproductive laborer, and it's important that he remain so if he doesn't want to end up as a pieceworker in the culture industry and mortgage his

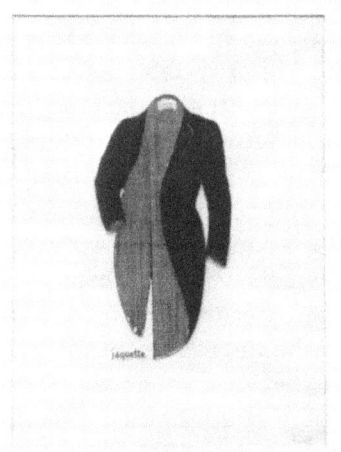 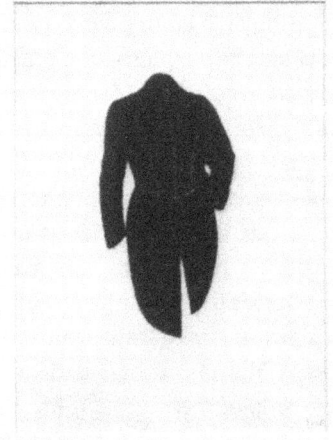

Marcel Duchamp, *Jaquette*, 1956. Private collection, New York. Photo Enrico Cattaneo. © 2012 Artists Rights Society (ARS), New York / ADAGP, Paris / Succession Marcel Duchamp

freedom. In other words, it is vital that he remain an artisan. Is that to say that he has to paint, to do handiwork, to "grind his chocolate himself"? Is that to say that he must resist the division of labor to the point of taking everything into his own hands, from the grinding of pigments all the way through the *vernissage*? Marx's artisan-tailor is unproductive because he works to order, because he is brought the cloth for the trousers and because it is his services that are paid for. This artisanship is a holdover from precapitalist relations of production. But if the artisan has his own cloth samples, if he has invested in a sewing machine, if he has his list of suppliers— and there is no lack of thread and weaving mills in Marx—he is already on the way to small business. In the same passage from *Capital*, Marx shows what artisanship has become or is in the process of becoming when it survives as an archaism walled off within the surrounding mode of production of industrial capitalism. He points out how the small artisan who works on commission sees, whether or not he wants to, whether or not he knows it, the social division of labor penetrating his own body and lives out his own activity in the mode of division, because separation of labor and capital is the dominant mode of social relations. He is a capitalist who owns his means of production, who employs himself as wage laborer, who buys his own labor power, who exploits his own overtime, and who pockets the surplus value thus created. The predictable outcome of this contradiction, Marx attests, is that either the artisan prospers, hiring workers and becoming a boss in his turn, or he fails, losing his means of production and ending up in the employ of someone else.

But this is not the situation of artists, or when it is, we stop talking of art in any ambitious sense. Their situation—and whatever they may do, whether they paint, write, compose, or are content to put the air they breathe in vials or to can other secretions of their labor power—is to lead, against all odds, the life of an independent artisan. This has nothing to do with what they make or with the craftsmanship of their work. It has hardly more to do with their suffering or their pleasure. Those who balk at the division will make it a point of honor to slick up their work all the while decrying the decline of tradition (these are the academicians). Those who find it intolerable to be divided will identify with the proletarian in themselves without seeing that the capitalist is to be found there as well, and will look for the reconciliation outside, for example in "social sculpture" (as did Beuys). Or if they are masochists they will identify with the capitalist, without seeing that they exploit the proletarian in themselves (as did Klein). And if they are really clever they will take their stakes out of the game by making themselves into a machine (as did Warhol). But all of that is beside the point. To lead the life of an artisan without suffering or pleasure, without promising or betraying, is to live one's life as an artist in the mode of division. It means casting away the pain of the artisan—who suffers from having to exploit himself if he wants to survive, from having to mess up the job to the point of losing the pleasure and pride he gets from his work, and from having to abandon traditional craftsmanship for makeshifts consuming less labor time—in a sort of existential *mise-en-abyme* for which Duchamp had the knack and through which he registered the division of labor that tears the artisan apart, separating him from himself: "Given that. . . . ; if I suppose I'm suffering a lot . . ." (This is in *The 1914 Box*, also.) When Duchamp gives up painting in 1912 and becomes a wageworker at the Ste. Geneviève Library "in order to paint for myself," he divides up the productive and unproductive laborers within himself. Up to that point it is nothing but a lifestyle; he has still to make a life out of it, and out of this life to make his oeuvre. Duchamp the employee makes no claim to art; Duchamp the artisan has stopped producing paintings. Registered: Mott's worker stakes no claim to art; Mutt the artisan no longer paints. Gone is the artisan-painter whose *Nude Descending a Staircase* and, even more, *Passage of the Virgin to the Bride* had shown his talent. Gone is tradition; gone is the nostalgic clinging to an outmoded craft pursued under hostile conditions. Coming up is "the *arrhe* of painting," in the singular and the feminine. And the question is, how does one make *Phynance* out of that?

Let's take up once again the fable of *la Fontaine* (for it's above all a moral tale, whereas creativity is a myth and the artist-machine a fiction): At the beginning of the story, Marcel Duchamp is R. Mutt, but this we won't know until the end. R. Mutt is like this Mr. Nobody who proclaims himself an artist in taking out his membership in the Society of Independent Artists; he divides himself into a stockholder and an artisan, Richard and Mutt. Richard is like Arensberg, both of them big stockholders in the society (both founding members) and both collectors (Richard is chair of the hanging committee and future founder of the Société Anonyme). Mutt is like Mott, artisan-painter or small industrialist. As artisan, Mutt suffers from having to separate his person into an exploited worker and a merchant who pockets the surplus value. As industrialist, Mott doesn't suffer, he exploits his workers. Mutt envies Mott and fears for his trade. For a year now, he hasn't stopped telling himself that he should paint (*qu'il peigne*),[2] but his *Chocolate Grinder* is already mortgaged and he is no longer anything but its *nominal* owner (says Marx). Feeling that he will soon have nothing but his creativity to sell, he withdraws his savings, stakes them all, and subcontracts. Mutt is once again like Mott, a merchant, alternately buyer and seller: Mott buys labor power and sells "items of lazy hardware," among which is a "faucet" that Mutt buys. At the end of the story Mutt has sold the "faucet" under a new label to Arensberg for a price virtually without a ceiling. Mott, who has gotten wind of the affair, just can't believe it. He gets after his workers with a prod, yet never can he extract such surplus value out of them. He shakes his head, muttering that even if he knows something about production, he understands nothing of *Phynance*. His workers have also gotten wind of the affair, and among them there is one who chuckles. On Sundays he paints "for himself," and for the modest sum of six dollars he took out his membership in the Independents. His name? R. Mutt.

Thus does Duchamp render unto Caesar that which is Caesar's: to Mott his means of production, which by nature are neither more nor less artistic than brushes and tubes of paint are for a painter; to Mott's workers their labor power, that is, their creativity, which is neither more nor less entitled to take the place that talent had in classical aesthetics than the Independents have the right to call themselves artists through wishful thinking; and to the modern artists their resistance to the destruction of their craft, which is neither more nor less justly defined by the technical specificity of the division of labor ("the bachelor grinds his chocolate himself") than by its social generality ("separation is an operation"). But Duchamp renders, as well: to Beuys the myth of creativity; to Warhol the fic-

2. Translator's note: the title of Duchamp's readymade *Peigne*, or *Comb*, is homophonic with the subjunctive of *peindre*, to paint.

tion of the machine; to Klein the emptiness of exchange value; and, need we add, to Marx what belongs to Marx. Yes, everyone is an artist; no, artists don't work; yes, the wish to proclaim oneself an artist is only a wish. Yes, the proletarians are alienated; yes, the relations of production are reified; yes, dialectical materialism claims that just practice proves the theory correct and vice versa. When the congruence between the aesthetic field and the field of political economy is perfect, there is nothing left by which to make this visible; but that proves nothing. It was up to Duchamp to show this congruence, and in showing it, he rendered to everyone what belonged to Duchamp. And he, what did he pocket? The fable isn't over. Who cashed Arensberg's blank check? Apparently no one; the check was fabulous in more senses than one. Duchamp, in any case, wanted to cash nothing, not even to take out the right to speculate on what he'd just made. Speculation had already taken place, and the profits had gone up in smoke. And when it would occur again, it would be for the benefit of Sidney Janis and Arturo Schwarz (who made replicas of *Fountain*), and for the pleasure of those art historians forced to speculate on what really happened with this "faucet which stops dripping when nobody is listening to it" but which—isn't that right, Marcel?—drips at the expense of those listening.

Fables are worth what they're worth, and this one isn't even supported. We don't know how things really happened, but at least we know that it wasn't like this. The urinal wasn't behind a partition and Arensberg didn't buy it. It was at Stieglitz's to be photographed, and the real Duchamp, less altruistic than the character in the fable, had certainly decided to draw interest on his investment. The question is to what extent we are speaking through "algebraic comparison" and to what extent *the arrhe of Phynance* has been superimposed on the art of finance. If the mapping of the two were perfectly congruent, then Duchamp would be nothing but an opportunist, cleverer than the others. Fables, after all, are worth what their moral is worth, and it is in the real world that the moral is tested. Thus we must find the counterproof to Arensberg's fabulous blank check. The *Tzanck Check* could be one. In December 1919, in Paris, Duchamp goes to his dentist, Daniel Tzanck, and pays for his care with a fictive check, wholly drawn by hand. Tzanck, who is also a collector and very active in Parisian avant-garde circles, knows very

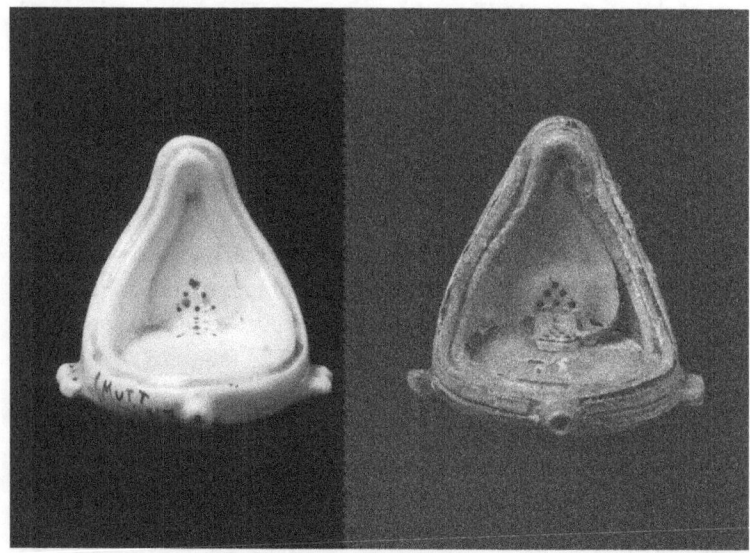

Marcel Duchamp: Left: *Fountain*, 1938, miniature urinal, glazed porcelain and paint, 4.5 × 6 × 8 cm. Right: *Fountain*, 1938, miniature urinal, papier-mâché, 4.5 × 6 × 8 cm. Photo: Galerie Tokoro, Tokyo. © 2012 Artists Rights Society (ARS), New York / ADAGP, Paris / Succession Marcel Duchamp

well what he is accepting for payment. In fact there are two transactions. Like any other dentist, Tzanck presents his bill and receives a check in return. But as a means of payment the check is worthless. Like the owner of the restaurant where Paul Klee ate for years in exchange for his paintings, he lets himself be paid "in kind," that is, in works of art. But this particular work of art is a check, and a check is not very gratifying when it comes to aesthetic pleasure. In accepting it the dentist renounces being paid; it is not exactly his services that he exchanges for money but the price of his services, already expressed in money, which he barters against a "Dada drawing" (as Picabia called it) not redeemable at the bank.

Duchamp obviously knows as well as Tzanck what he is proposing for payment. He suspects that if Tzanck—like Klee's restaurant owner, no doubt—accepts a work of art in payment for his care, this is not only because the art lover in him, the craftsman who knows what work well done means, has instinctively recognized the fine workmanship of the drawing the artist offers him, but also because the collector in him has instinctively recognized the speculative potential of the deal. Indeed, doesn't Duchamp suggest to him that a bank exists where the *Tzanck Check* is redeemable? It is the one on which it is drawn, The Teeth's Loan & Trust Company, Consolidated, which lists its legal address as 2 Wall Street, New York. Here we can savor Duchamp's marvelous humor. In inventing a New York bank (a strange thing since we're in Paris), he cloaks with English the fact that the name of the bank articulates exactly the nature of the exchange and of the complicity that forms between the two men: "I loan you my teeth, and in return you give me your trust, and thus will our relations be consolidated."

For twenty years the check stayed in the dentist's collection. During these twenty years Duchamp breathed, played chess, took part in a surrealist exhibition here and there, and, discreetly but not apologetically, served as a broker. He sold an impressive number of works of modern art, many his own, to various people including Arensberg, his sidekick since the Richard Mutt affair. The war was approaching, and the moment came to pack his (*boîte en*) valise. In 1940 he tried to interest Arensberg in the *Tzanck Check*—drawn up in 1919 for $115.00—even writing to him that his dentist "would be delighted to accept $50.00 to send it to you." So much for finance:

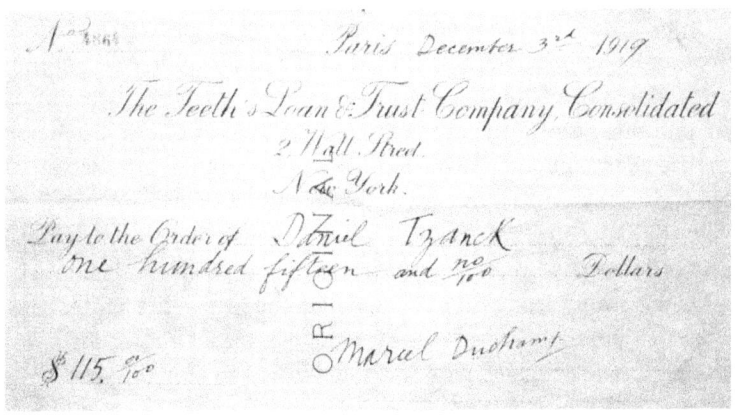

Marcel Duchamp, *Chèque Tzanck*, 1919. © 2012 Artists Rights Society (ARS), New York / ADAGP, Paris / Succession Marcel Duchamp

quite a shark, this Duchamp, when it was a matter of playing go-between for two of his collectors. Perhaps Tzanck had not been faithful enough to him (he owned only one other work by him, as chance would have it an investment of the same type, to wit, the *Monte Carlo Bond*). Arensberg apparently didn't want the check. Duchamp then approached Daniel Tzanck and bought the check back "for a lot more than it says it's worth." So much for *Phynance*: the artist had paid his dentist's bill in full, but as a check to be guaranteed on trust, the *arrhe* required the balance.

The moral of a fable isn't dissipated in the real world, it returns to the world of fables through *symétrie commanditée*. This is Duchamp's expression, and it brings finance back to *Phynance*. A *commandite* is an investment in a joint-stock company with liability only for the sum invested. And a *société en commandite* is a commercial enterprise formed of two sorts of partners; the first (the investing silent partners) bring capital without taking part in the running of the company; the others (those invested) are jointly responsible for all legal debts. In Duchamp's limited partnership, we once again meet up with all the characters from the fable, as from real life: Richard/Arensberg investing in Mutt/Mott, and symmetrically, Duchamp investing in Tzanck. When he buys the check back from him, he is not liable for any possible losses on the dentist's part. Arensberg has been the fabulous investor, right from the beginning. It is only fair that the one who had offered a virtually limitless price for a urinal he never possessed should assemble his protégé's work as completely as possible. But the latter is caught up in still another enterprise: a *commandite* is also a typesetters' collective working by the job. One month before making up the *Tzanck Check*, Duchamp put the character sequence L.H.O.O.Q. in his composing stick in order to title a somewhat mustachioed reproduction of the *Mona Lisa*. Now the typesetter needs the *Tzanck Check* to have it reproduced for the *Boîte en valise*. He has understood how profitable it would be to keep his complete works to himself in the form—the lightest and most easily tradable form—of a portable museum composed of reproductions. For Arensberg, the gold in the safe; for Duchamp, the fiat money backed up by it. The artist coins money on the "Arensberg Bank," or on the "Mary Sisler Bank"—in short, he runs off reproductions of the works that his most faithful collectors have accumulated the way others write checks on their bank accounts. And

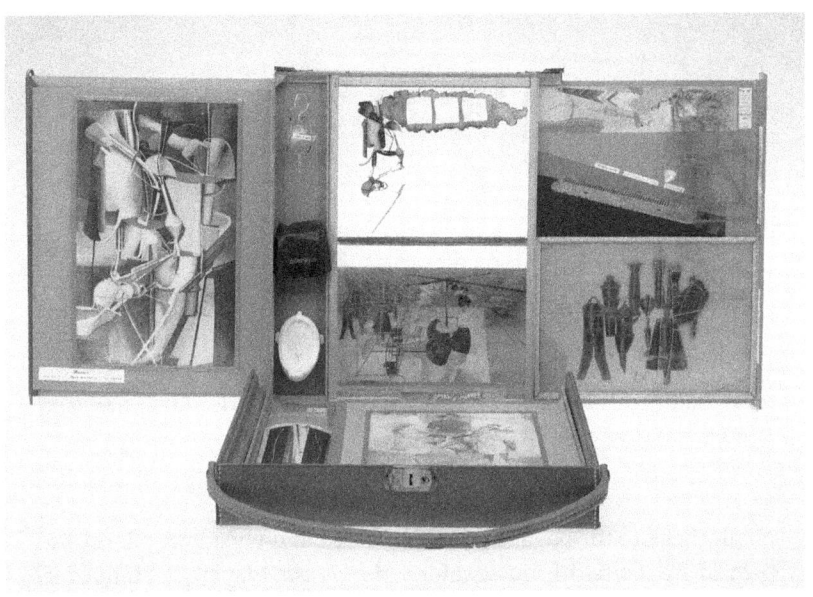

Marcel Duchamp, *Boîte-en-Valise*, 1941. Philadelphia Museum of Art, Louise and Walter Arensberg Collection. Photo: The Philadelphia Museum of Art / Art Resource, NY. © 2012 Artists Rights Society (ARS), New York / ADAGP, Paris / Succession Marcel Duchamp

this is how all the *symétries commanditées* will be fulfilled and how that which belongs to Caesar will be rendered unto Caesar.

It's a certain Phillip Bruno who in 1965 cashed Arensberg's fabulous check. The event took place during the exhibition of Mary Sisler's collection at Cordier & Ekstrom (*Not Seen and/or Less Seen of/by Marcel Duchamp/Rrose Sélavy, 1904-1964*). L.H.O.O.Q. was included in the show, echoed—through *symétrie commanditée*—by the *shaved Mona Lisa* that served as the invitation to the opening. The *Tzanck Check* was there as well, having in the meantime traveled from Duchamp's wallet to those of Patricia Matta, Arne Ekstrom, and finally Mary Sisler. The story doesn't tell whether Phillip Bruno collected anything besides reproductions; in any case the fact remains that he made the catalogue into an album into which, without covering over the photographs, he pasted all the press clippings about the exhibition he could gather. He wished to obtain a Duchamp autograph, and with a paper clip he whimsically attached a

Marcel Duchamp, *Chèque Bruno*, 1965. © 2012 Artists Rights Society (ARS), New York / ADAGP, Paris / Succession Marcel Duchamp

blank check to the page where the reproduction of *Tzanck Check* appeared, opposite the mustachioed *Mona Lisa*. Playing the innocent, he presented Duchamp with the book opened to the page in question, awaiting his autograph. Of course Duchamp signed the check for him, filling in the amount: "unlimited"; and the bank (French this time although we're in New York): "Banque Mona Lisa."

The Mona Lisa Bank is the Louvre. Every artist, even and above all the *enfant terrible* of the avant-garde, writes checks on tradition. They have the value only of that with which tradition gets repaid. For the *arrhe* of painting, posterity will pay the balance, if it has enough of a sense of humor. The *Mona Lisa*, with and without mustaches, belongs to it. The artist has put his papers in order and organized his estate: to Leonardo the painting, and to the culture industry the right to print it on T-shirts; to Rrose the enigmatic smile, and to Mona the hot pants; to the cut-up Georges Hugnet the mustaches, and to Marcel Duchamp the razor blades that have "cuttage" in reserve. He could recall that his only utopia had been to "establish a society in which the individual has to pay for the air he breathes," and now leaves to his creditors the bother of "cutting off the air in case of nonpayment." He himself thinks that he has breathed enough. On October 2, 1968, age takes charge of quietly blowing out the candle. *Sélavy* (*c'est la vie*), right?—*besides, it's always the others who die.*

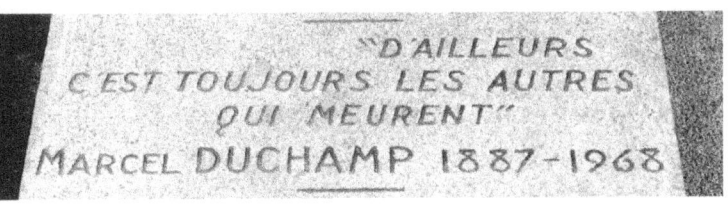

Duchamp's *Grave: D'ailleurs c'est toujours les autres qui meurent* (Besides it's always the others who die), epitaph on Duchamp's tomb, Rouen cemetery

Postface 2009

In 1988, the perfect mapping of aesthetics onto political economy yielded this book. May it stand or fall on its own merits. I wouldn't write the same book today, but I still adhere to the thesis it defends, and the quibbles I have with its style are not decisive. I wouldn't even change a comma to the infamous chapter on Yves Klein that caused the manuscript to be rejected by its commissioner, although I have drastically revised my appreciation of Klein's work. This is either a contradiction (that needs to be solved) or a mystery (that is best left untouched), I can't decide.

It is a contradiction if you think that the moral conduct of artists, their convictions and beliefs, and their positioning on the ideological or the political spectrum affect the quality of their work. It is a mystery if you think they do not. I can't decide that either, because I don't have a general rule applicable to all artists. For example, the quality of Mondrian's painting seems to me absolutely independent of the artist's theosophical convictions, let alone his corny gender theory (whereby vertical lines are masculine and horizontal lines feminine). A feminist critique of Mondrian would not affect the art. He probably needed those beliefs in order to paint what he painted, but the paintings, in order to be appreciated as paintings, never call on them, or on any belief whatever, on the part of the viewer. In the chapter on Joseph Beuys, I didn't judge his sculpture by the yardstick of his equally corny economic theory. Why, then, did I systematically take Yves Klein at his own word? Did I not use my eyes? And why do I still endorse my text today, now that I have revised my appreciation of Klein's work?

I was using my eyes in 1988. The text I wrote was not based solely on scholarship; it relied on the memory of many scattered experiences of Klein's works here and there, most notably in Krefeld, where a significant body of his work is assembled; and it relied even more heavily on my memory of the 1983 retrospective at the Pompidou Center, curated by Jean-Yves Mock. The show had something macabre about it that made the works appear, in conformity with what Klein had said, as "the ashes of [his] art," indeed. If I remember well, *Here Lies Space*, the first work my text mentions, was prominently displayed in the first room. A tombstone thus proposed itself as a key to the entire oeuvre. Ironically, it was another Klein retrospective at the Pompidou Center, this time curated by Camille Morineau in 2006, which completely overturned my perception of the work. It was at least as comprehensive as the 1983 show (something that isn't reflected in a comparison of the two catalogues), and it covered all aspects of Klein's work and life equally well, if not better. But the emphasis was on the paintings, several of which I had never seen before. Their diversity, especially in the *Monogold* and the *Monopink* registers, not forgetting the *Anthropométries* and the very radical *Peintures de Feu*, was stunning; they were alive with vibrant energy, and the best ones withstood critical comparison with anything abstract expressionist and color field painters have produced; the way they were installed gave them plenty of space to breathe, and they deserved that space. Klein himself may have seen them as ashes; to me they were more like the phoenix rising from them.

The rest of his work, strangely enough, benefited from the light the paintings threw on it. The *Yves, Peintures* artist's book, the exhibition of the void, the *Journal du Dimanche*, even the selling of the *Zones of Pictorial Sensibility* seemed less anticipations of conceptual art than acts of faith through which Klein had mustered the determination and energy to keep on painting. I know that some critics will hold precisely that against him, reproaching him for not having understood that his own advances in the direction of performance and institutional critique had made painting obsolete once and for all. The same critics, I suppose, will deem me conservative for rehabilitating Klein for the quality of his paintings. But if they admit seeing that quality like me, the burden of proof is on them: Why must the very fact that Klein kept painting till the end of his life be interpreted as a contradiction, incoherence, or lack of radicality in view of his other work? Why can it not be seen as the very coherent practice of a man who intimately knew he was a painter because of what and how he painted, and in spite of his also very coherent, if perverse, intelligence in the modern mapping of aesthetics onto political economy? After all, the brand of spiritualism that leads one to think of painting in terms of "immaterial pictorial sensibility" is no more ridiculous than the theosophy espoused by Mondrian. To use women as "living brushes" may be reprehensible from a feminist point of view, but it is definitely less corny than thinking of vertical and horizontal lines as gendered according to the most hackneyed male cliché. (Incidentally: I was struck by Klein's utter respect for the nude models of his *Anthropométries* in the film footage presented in the show.) All things considered, I don't find it impossible to look at Klein's work the way I look at Mondrian's: its quality is such that it is not affected by his superstitious religiosity, his histrionic behavior, or his decidedly unethical claim to appropriate the means of artistic production. Thus I feel free to call Yves Klein a major artist without having to change a comma (well, maybe a comma) in the chapter on him in this book.

www.ingramcontent.com/pod-product-compliance
Lightning Source LLC
Chambersburg PA
CBHW061443180526
45170CB00004B/1537

* 9 7 8 0 2 2 6 9 2 2 3 8 6 *